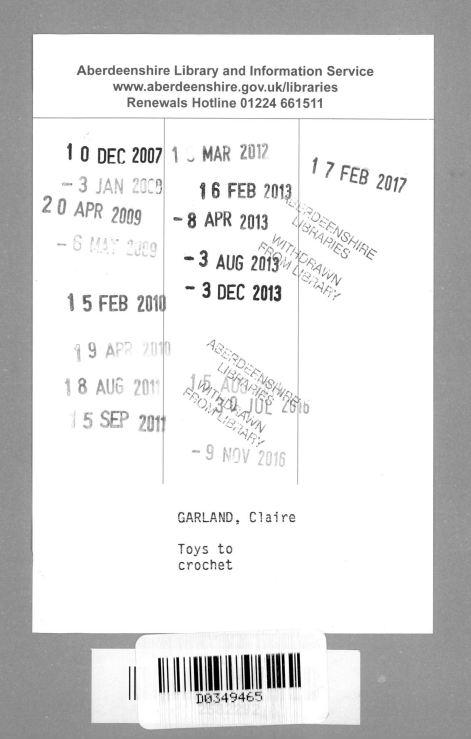
GARLAND, Claire

Toys to
crochet

toys to crochet

toys to crochet

Claire Garland

COLLINS & BROWN

First published in the United Kingdom in 2007 by
Collins & Brown
10 Southcombe Street
London
W14 0RA

An imprint of Anova Books Company Ltd

Commissioning Editor: Michelle Lo
Design Manager: Gemma Wilson
Assistant Editor: Katie Hudson
Design Studios: Ben Cracknell
Photographer: Mark Winwood
Senior Production Controller: Morna McPherson

ISBN 978-1-84340-400-2

A CIP catalogue for this book is available from the
British Library.

10 9 8 7 6 5 4 3 2 1

Reproduction by Spectrum Colour Ltd, Ipswich
Printed and bound by SNP Leefung, China

This book can be ordered direct from the publisher.
Contact the marketing department, but try your
bookshop first.

www.anovabooks.com

Contents

Introduction

I've always found crochet to be a craft of myriad benefits. On a professional level, it's a design tool that provides ease and workability – after all, what other craft allows one to create perfect circles in a matter of a few simple knots? On a personal note, crocheting is a stress-reliever and an ideal way to unwind after a long day. With just a hook and a ball of yarn, crocheting offers an immediate sense of accomplishment and release, especially when creating toys.

My creative inspiration is sparked by my children – I observe the way they create miniature worlds and how their toys develop into 'loveable friends' and 'cuddly beasts'. My objective in this book was to create a collection of unique and character-driven toys, like the pint-sized projects in *Toys to Knit* and *Toys to Sew*. The results, I hope, are fun creations that are totally endearing.

I couldn't possibly choose a favourite from the projects – they all brim with personality, and I love them equally. The Mermaid, with her cascading mane and long, crocheted fin, radiates beauty; the Marmoset, in his red overalls, is always up for mischief; and George the Shark may *look* mean, but he's really a soft-hearted guy.

All the projects in *Toys to Crochet* are easy to make and require very little time to finish, which is great when you have an anxious child peering over your shoulder. (I recommend stitching up a couple of finger puppets for such an occasion!)

I hope the projects in this book bring as much satisfaction to you as they have for me. I thoroughly enjoyed designing and making each toy, and I hope I've managed to express this pleasure on every page.

Enjoy and get hooked!

Dolls &
Doll Clothes

This chapter contains patterns for a doll, a basic bear with a variety of clothes, and several adorable accessories. Once you have conquered the basics, take your pick from this collection of lovable projects.

Basic Bear

This classic bear can be crocheted up without a hitch. Use him as the foundation for Sailor Bear (page 27) – or combine him with other basic clothes to create your own unique teddy.

FINISHED SIZE
31 cm (12¼ in) tall × 35 cm (13¾ in) wide (arms outstretched)

MATERIALS
- **Karabella *Aurora Bulky*** One ball Beige 22 (MC)
- Hook: 5.00 mm (H-8)
- Black embroidery thread for attaching beads and for mouth
- Two 6 mm (¼ in) black glass pearls or similar for eyes
- Dark blue embroidery thread for nose
- Polyester toy fibrefill or wadding
- Yarn needle

TENSION
9 sts and 8 rnds measured over 5 cm (2 in), working double crochet in MC and using 5.00 mm (H-8) hook.

NOTE:
Before beg the second rnd in each section, place a marker or short length of contrasting yarn across your crochet and up against the loop on the hook and above the working yarn. Work Rnd 2, then slip the marker out and place it at the beg of the next rnd and so on. The marker will indicate where each subsequent rnd starts.

HEAD
Foundation row: Beg at the nose end and using MC, make 2ch.
Rnd 1: 8dc in 2nd ch from hook.
Rnd 2: [1dc in each of next 2dc, 2dc in next dc] twice, 1dc in each of next 2dc (10 dc).
Rnd 3: 1dc in each dc around.
Shape top of nose
Rnd 4: [1dc in each of next 2dc, 2dc in next dc] 3 times, 1dc in next dc (13 dc).
Rnd 5: 1dc in each dc around.
Rnd 6: *2dc in each dc around (26 dc).
Rnd 7: 1dc in each dc around.
Rnd 8: [1dc in each of next 3dc, 2dc in next dc] 5 times, 1dc in next 6dc (31 dc).
Rnd 9: 1dc in each dc around.
Shape back of head
Rnd 10: Miss first dc, *1dc in each of next 4dc, miss next dc, rep from * to end (24 dc).
Rnd 11: 1dc in each dc around.
Rnd 12: *1dc in each of next 3dc, miss next dc, rep from * to end (18 dc).
Rnd 13: *1dc in each of next 2dc, miss next dc, rep from * to end (12 dc).
Turn out to RS. Stuff the head lightly.
Rnd 14: *1dc in next dc, miss next dc, rep from * to end (6 dc).
Rep last row until gap is closed. Fasten off. Weave in end.

EARS
Make 2 alike.
Foundation row: Beg at the ear base and using MC, make 2ch.
Row 1: 6dc in 2nd ch from hook, turn.
Row 2: 1ch, 1dc in top half of each dc along.
Fasten off, leaving a tail end long enough with which to hand-sew the ears onto the head.

BODY
Foundation row: Beg at the bottom and using MC, make 4ch, join with sl st at the top of first ch to make a ring.
Rnd 1: 12htr in ring.
Rnd 2: 1htr in each htr around.
Rnd 3: *1htr in next htr, 2htr in next htr, rep from * to end (18 htr).
Rnd 4: 1htr in each htr around.
Rep last 2 rnds once more (27 htr).
Rnd 7: 1htr in each htr around.
Shape back
Rnd 8: [1htr in next htr, miss next htr]

5 times, 1htr in each of next 17 htr
(22 htr).

Rnd 9: [1htr in next htr, miss next htr]
4 times, 1htr in each of next 11 htr
(18 htr).

Rnd 10: 1htr in each htr around.
Rep last rnd once more.

Rnd 12: *1htr in next htr, miss next htr,
rep from * to end (9 htr).
Stuff the body.

Rnd 13: *1htr in each of next 2htr, miss
next htr, rep from * to end (6 htr).
Fasten off, leaving a tail end long
enough to join the body to the head.

ARMS

Make 2 alike.

Foundation row (RS): Beg at the top of
the arm and using MC, make 21ch.

Row 1 (WS): 1dc in 2nd ch from hook,
1dc in each ch to end, turn (20 dc).

Row 2 (RS): 1ch, 1dc in each dc to end,
turn (20 dc).
Rep last row 3 times more.

Shape hand

Row 6 (RS): 1ch, 1dc in each of next
6dc, turn.

Row 7 (WS): 1ch, miss next dc, 1dc in
each dc across, turn (5 dc).

Row 8 (RS): 1ch, miss next dc, 1dc in each dc across, turn (4 dc).

Row 9 (WS): 1ch, miss next dc, 1dc in next dc, miss next dc, 1dc in next dc (3 dc). Fasten off, leaving a tail end long enough for you to sew the arm seam.

Join other half of hand

With RS facing and working along foundation row edge, count in 6ch from hand end, pull though yarn MC to 6th ch, 1ch, 1dc in each ch to end (6 dc).

Row 2 (WS): 1ch, miss next dc, 1dc in each dc across, turn (5 dc).

Row 3 (RS): 1ch, miss next dc, 1dc in each dc across, turn (4 dc).

Row 4 (WS): 1ch, miss next dc, 1dc in next dc, miss next dc, 1dc in next dc (2 dc). Fasten off.

LEGS

Make 2 alike.

Foundation row: Beg at toe and using MC, make 2ch.

Rnd 1: 6dc in 2nd ch from hook.

Rnd 2: *1dc in next dc, 2dc in next dc, rep from * around (9 dc).

Rnd 3: 1dc in each dc around. Rep last rnd 5 times more.

Shape heel

Row 9: 1dc in each of next 4dc, turn.

Row 10: 1ch, 1dc in each of next 4dc, turn.

Rep last row once more.

Fasten off. Join heel seam – fold the finishing row (last 4dc) in half so that the two ends meet and sew together to form back of heel.

Shape top of foot

Rnd 1: Join in yarn MC with a sl st at top of heel seam, work 4dc along first row-end edge of heel, 1dc in each of 5dc across front of foot, then 4dc along 2nd row-end edge of heel (13 dc).

Rnd 2: 1dc in each of next 13dc.

Shape ankle

Rnd 3: [1dc in each of next 3dc, miss next dc] 3 times, 1dc in next dc (10 dc).

Rnd 4: 1dc in each of next 10dc. Rep last rnd until the leg measures 19 cm (7½ in) from toe. Fasten off.

TO FINISH

Referring to the photograph for the positioning of eyes, hand sew a bead on either side of the nose. Using dark blue embroidery thread, hand sew the nose with a few horizontal stitches. Sew a mouth using six strands of black embroidery thread by securing a length of thread at the corner of the mouth position at the back of the face, bring the thread to the front, re-inserting at the length you want the mouth to be. Sew a short stitch in the middle of the stitched line, securing the stitch down.

Stuff the body fairly firmly. Close the gap at the bottom. Hand-sew the head to the body. Oversew the arms to join, stuffing the hands lightly.

Stuff the feet. Sew the arms to the side of the body and the legs to the bottom. Sew the ears to the top of the head. If you wish, you can hand-sew a button (10 mm (³/₈ in) in diameter) to the back of the bear's waist. This will help to hold up the trousers, pants and skirt. The button needs to be small enough to go through a dc stitch, yet large enough to secure the garments.

Basic Doll

This pattern is the foundation for all dolls in the book. Dress her in the Basic Clothes (page 16) or Sun Clothes (page 21) – a stylish ensemble proves that being short on stature doesn't mean being short on taste!

FINISHED SIZE
42 cm (16½ in) tall × 50 cm (19¾ in) wide (arms outstretched)

MATERIALS
- **Rooster Yarns** *Almerino DK*
  One ball Cornish 201 (MC)
- **DK medium (light worsted/worsted weight)** of your choice
  One ball in a suitable hair colour (A)
- **Debbie Bliss** *Baby Cashmerino*
  One ball Baby Blue 340204 for tankini (B)
- Hooks: 3.50 mm (E-4) and 4.00 mm (G-6)
- Small pieces of felt for eyes
- Black thread for sewing on eyes
- Two 6 mm (¼ in) black glass beads or similar for eyes
- Pink embroidery thread for sewing mouth
- Polyester toy fibrefill or wadding
- Yarn needle

TENSION
For doll: 12 sts and 12 rnds measured over 5 cm (2 in), working double crochet in MC and using 3.50 mm (E-4) hook.

For undergarments: 9 sts and 10 rows measured over 5 cm (2 in), working double crochet in B and using 4.00 mm (G-6) hook.

NOTE:
Before beg the second rnd in each section, place a marker or short length of contrasting yarn across your crochet and up against the loop on the hook and above the working yarn. Work Rnd 2 then slip the marker out and place it at the beg of the next rnd and so on. The marker will indicate where each subsequent rnd starts.

HEAD & BODY
Make back and front alike.
Foundation row: Using yarn MC and 3.50 mm (E-4) hook, beg at the base, make 13ch.
Row 1: 1dc in 2nd ch from hook, 1dc in each ch across, turn (12 dc).
Row 2: 2ch, 1dc in 2nd ch from hook, 1dc in each dc to last dc, 2dc in last dc, turn (14 dc).
Row 3: 1ch, 1dc in each dc across, turn. Rep last 2 rows twice more (18 dc).

Row 8: 1ch, 1dc in each of next 18 dc, turn (18 dc).
Rep last row 8 times more.

Shape body and neck
Row 17: 1ch, miss first dc, 1dc in each dc to last 2dc, miss next dc, 1dc in last dc, turn (16 dc).
Rep last row 3 times more (10 dc).
Row 21: 1ch, 1dc in each dc across, turn (10 dc).
Rep last row 5 times more.

Shape head
Row 27: 2ch, 1dc in 2nd ch from hook, 1dc in each dc to last dc, 2dc in last dc, turn (12 dc).
Rep last row twice more (16 dc).
Row 30: 1ch, 1dc in each dc across, turn (16 dc).
Rep last row 3 times more.

Shape top of head
Row 34: 1ch, miss first dc, 1dc in each dc to last 2dc, miss next dc, 1dc in last dc, turn (14 dc).
Rep last row 4 times more (6 dc).
Fasten off.

ARMS
Make 2 alike.
Foundation row: Using yarn MC and 3.50 mm (E-4) hook, make 38ch.
Row 1: 1dc in 2nd ch from hook, 1dc in each ch across, turn (37 dc).

Row 2: 1ch, 1dc in each dc across, turn (37 dc).
Rep last row twice more.
Fasten off, leaving a long tail end – use this to oversew along the foundation and finishing rows to join.

FEET & LEGS
Make 2 alike.
Foundation row: Using yarn MC and 3.50 mm (E-4) hook, beg at toe, make 2ch.
Rnd 1: 6dc in 2nd ch from hook.
Rnd 2: *1dc in next dc, 2dc in next dc, rep from * around (9 dc).
Rnd 3: 1dc in each of next 9dc.
Rep last rnd 5 times more.

Shape heel
Row 1: 1dc in each of next 4dc, turn.
Row 2: 1ch, 1dc in each of next 4dc, turn.
Rep last row once more.
Fasten off. Join heel seam – fold the finishing row (last 4dc) in half so that the two ends meet and sew together to form back of heel.

Shape top of foot
Rnd 1: Join in yarn MC with a sl st at top of heel seam, work 4dc along first row-end edge of heel, 1dc in each of 5dc across front of foot, then 4dc along 2nd row-end edge of heel (13 dc).
Rnd 2: 1dc in each of next 13dc.

Shape ankle
Rnd 3: [1dc in each of next 3dc, miss next dc] 3 times, 1dc in last dc, turn (10 dc).
Stuff the foot.
Rnd 4: 1dc in each of next 10dc.
Rep last rnd until the leg measures 23 cm (9 in) from toe.
Fasten off.

TO FINISH
Cut out two circles from felt 10 mm (3/8 in) in diameter for the irises.
Sew a bead to the centre of each iris. Referring to the photograph for positioning, sew the eyes to the face. Sew a mouth using six strands of pink embroidery thread by securing a length of yarn at the corner of the mouth position at the back of the face and bring the yarn to the front, reinsert at desired mouth length. Sew a short stitch in the middle of the stitched line, securing the stitch down a little to form the bottom lip. Work another stitch above this 'caught' stitch to form the upper lip.
Using a blunt-ended yarn needle and yarn MC, join the front of the body to the back, leaving the bottom edge open for stuffing. Stuff the doll firmly in the head, and very lightly in the trunk. Close the gap at the bottom.

Oversew the arms to join. Sew the arms to the side of the body.

Sew the legs to the bottom of the body. To sew on hair, cut yarn A into lengths of 36 cm (14¼ in). Taking one length at a time, bend it in half and, using a crochet hook, pull the loop through a dc stitch at the top of the head, referring to the photograph for hair placement. Pass the cut ends through the loops, then pull the cut ends firmly so that the knot lies at the top of the head. Continue with this fringing technique along the top and a little way down the back of the head, depending on how thick you want the hair to be.

Tankini

BOTTOM

Foundation row: Using yarn B and 4.00 mm (G-6) hook, make 33ch.
Row 1: 1dc in 2nd ch from hook, 1dc in each ch across, turn (32 dc).
Row 2: 1ch, 1dc in each of next 32dc, join into ring with sl st in first dc, taking care not to twist the rows (32 dc).
Cont to work in rnds.
Rnd 1: 1dc in each dc around (32 dc).
Rep last rnd twice more.
Shape front
Row 1: 1dc in each of next 12dc, turn (12 dc).
Row 2: 1ch, 1dc in each of next 12dc, turn.
Row 3: 1ch, miss first dc, 1dc in each of next 9dc, miss next dc, 1dc in last dc, turn (10 dc).
Row 4: 1ch, 1dc in each of next 10dc, turn (10 dc).
Row 5: 1ch, miss first dc, 1dc in each of next 7dc, miss next dc, 1dc in last dc, turn (8 dc).
Row 6: 1ch, 1dc in each of next 8dc, turn (8 dc).
Row 7: 1ch, miss first dc, 1dc in each of next 5dc, miss next dc, 1dc in last dc, turn (6 dc).
Row 8: 1ch, 1dc in each of next 6dc, turn (6 dc).
Row 9: 1ch, miss first dc, 1dc in each of next 3dc, miss next dc, 1dc in last dc, turn (4 dc).
Row 10: 1ch, 1dc in each of next 4dc (4 dc).
Fasten off, leaving a long tail end for sewing up the gusset seam.
Shape back
Row 1: With RS facing, join in yarn B to first of 20 rem dc at left back, 1ch, miss dc where yarn was joined, 1dc in each of next 17dc, miss next dc, 1dc in last dc, turn (18 dc).
Row 2: 1ch, miss first dc, 1dc in each to last dc, miss last dc, turn (16 dc).
Rep last row 6 times more, turn (4 dc).
Row 9: 1ch, 1dc in each of next 4dc.
Fasten off, weave in loose end.

TO FINISH

With RS facing and matching yarn, sew up the short waist seam and gusset seam, leaving the legs open.

TOP

Foundation row: Using yarn B and 4.00 mm (G-6) hook, make 18ch, turn.
Row 1: 1dc in 2nd ch from hook, 1dc in each ch across, turn (17 dc).
Row 2: 1ch, 1dc in each of next 17dc, turn.
Row 3: 1ch, 1 dc in first dc, *miss 1dc, 5tr in next dc, miss 1dc, 1dc in next dc, rep from * to end.
Fasten off.
For the back strap, make a chain long enough to fit across the back and sew to row-ends of the top.
For each shoulder strap, make a chain long enough to fit over the shoulders. Sew one end of each strap to the foundation row of the top and the other end to the back strap.

Basic Clothes

A fashionable girl-about-town needs a chic urban wardrobe to reflect her unique personality. Many of these garments are the basics for other clothes within this chapter. A hat and striped culottes look fabulous day and night, while a button-up hoodie is ideal outerwear when the temperature drops.

Hooded Cardigan

FINISHED SIZE
20 × 24 cm (8 × 9½ in) from bottom to tip of hood

MATERIALS
- **Sirdar** *Snuggly DK*
  One ball of Lilac 219 (MC)
- **Anchor** *Tapisserie Wool*
  One ball of Damson 8512 for button band (A)
- Hook: 5.00 mm (H-8)
- Three 18 mm (¾ in) buttons
- Yarn needle

TENSION
9 sts and 7 rows measured over 5 cm (2 in), working double crochet in MC and using 5.00 mm (H-8) hook.

NOTE:
Before beg the second rnd in each section, place a marker or short length of contrasting yarn across your crochet and up against the loop on the hook and above the working yarn. Work Rnd 2

then slip the marker out and place it at the beg of the next rnd and so on. The marker will indicate where each subsequent rnd starts.

FRONT
Foundation row: Beg at right centre front, and using yarn A, make 12ch.
Row 1 (RS): 2dc in 2nd ch from hook, 1dc in each ch across, turn (12 dc).
Row 2: 1ch, 1dc in first dc, (miss next 2dc, make buttonhole by making 2ch, 1dc in each of next 2dc) twice, miss next 2dc, make 2ch, 2dc in last dc, turn (13 sts).
Row 3: Join in yarn MC with a sl st in last dc of previous row, 1ch, 2dc in first dc, 1dc in next dc, 2dc in next 2ch sp, (1dc in each of next 2dc, 2dc in next 2ch sp) twice, 1dc in last dc, turn (14 dc).
Row 4: 1ch, 1dc in each dc across, turn.
Row 5: 1ch, 2dc in first dc, 1dc in each dc across, turn (15 dc).
Row 6: 1ch, 1dc in each dc across, turn. Rep last row 3 times more.
Make right armhole
Row 10 (WS): 1ch, 1dc in each of next 6dc, miss next 7dc, make 7ch, 1dc in each

of next 2dc, turn.
Make back
Row 11 (RS): 1ch, 1dc in each of next 2dc, 1dc in each of next 7ch, 1dc in each of next 6dc, turn.
Row 12: 1ch, 1dc in each dc across, turn. Rep last row 8 times more.
Make left armhole
Row 21 (RS): 1ch, 1dc in each of next 2dc, miss next 7dc, make 7ch, 1dc in each of next 6dc, turn.
Row 22: 1ch, 1dc in each of next 6dc, 1dc in each of next 7ch, 1dc in each of next 2dc, turn (15 dc).
Row 23: 1ch, 1dc in each dc across, turn. Rep last row 3 times more.
Row 27 (RS): Sl st in first dc, 1ch, 1dc in each dc across, turn (14 dc).
Row 28: 1ch, 1dc in each dc to last dc, miss last dc, turn (13 dc). Rep last 2 rows once more.
Row 31 (RS): Sl st in first dc, 1ch, 1dc in each dc across (10 dc). Fasten off.

SLEEVES

Make 2 alike.

Rnd 1: With RS facing, join yarn MC with a sl st into a dc at base of armhole and drawing a loop through, make 1ch, 1dc in each dc along edges of armhole, join with sl st in top of first dc, turn (14 dc).

Rnd 2: Working from the inside of the cardigan, 1ch, 1dc in each of next 14 dc. Rep last rnd until the entire sleeve – from Rnd 1 – measures 8 cm (3 in), ending with a sl st in top of first dc.
Fasten off and weave in ends.

HOOD

Row 1: With RS facing, join on MC with a sl st into the dc at beg of right centre front and, drawing a loop through, make 1ch, work 30dc along neck edge to left centre front, turn.

Row 2: Sl st in first dc, 1ch, 1dc in each of next 27dc, miss next dc, 1dc in last dc, turn (28 dc).

Row 3: 1ch, 1dc in each dc across, turn.

Row 4: Sl st in first dc, 1ch, 1dc in each of next 25dc, miss next dc, 1dc in last dc, turn (26 dc).

Row 5: 1ch, 1dc in each dc across, turn.

Row 6: Sl st in first dc, 1ch, 1dc in each of next 23dc, miss next dc, 1dc in last dc, turn (24 dc).

Row 7: 1ch, 1dc in each dc across, turn. Rep last row 4 times more.

Row 12: 1ch, 1dc in each of next 11dc, [2dc in next dc] twice, 1dc in each of next 11dc, turn (26 dc).

Row 13: 1ch, 1dc in each dc across, turn.

Row 14: 1ch, 1dc in each of next 12dc, [2dc in next dc] twice, 1dc in each of next 12dc, turn (28 dc).

Row 15: 1ch, 1dc in each dc across, turn.

Row 16: 1ch, 1dc in each of next 13dc, [2dc in next dc] twice, 1dc in each of next 13dc, turn (30 dc).

Row 17: 1ch, 1dc in each dc across, turn.

Row 18: 1ch, 1dc in each of next 14dc, [2dc in next dc] twice, 1dc in each of next 14dc, turn (32 dc).

Row 19: 1ch, 1dc in each dc across. Fasten off, leaving a tail end long enough to sew up the seam with. With RS facing,

sew up the hood along the finishing row. Weave in end.

HOOD EDGING

With RS facing, join in yarn A with a sl st into the last dc worked at end of button band and, drawing a loop through, make 1ch, 1dc in each row-end edge along hood edge to left centre front, ending in sl st in top of last dc. Fasten off.

Basic Trousers

FINISHED SIZE

17 cm (6¾ in) long and 23 cm (9 in) in diameter around waist

MATERIALS

- **Rooster** *Almerino DK*
  One ball of Caviar 206 (MC)
  One ball of Hazelnut 202 (A)
- Hook size: 5.00 mm (H-8)
- 30 cm (12 in) × 6 mm (¼ in) ribbon for waist tie

TENSION

8 sts and 9 rows measured over 5 cm (2 in), working double crochet in MC and using 5.00 mm (H-8) hook.

TROUSERS

Follow this colour sequence throughout the pattern:
Foundation row and Row 1 – yarn MC.
Rows 2 and 3 – yarn A.
Rows 4 and 5 – yarn MC.
Rows 6 and 7 – yarn A, and so on.
Foundation row: Using yarn MC, beg at the leg end, make 27ch.
Row 1: 1dc in 2nd ch from hook, 1dc in each ch across, turn (26 dc).
Row 2: 1ch, 1dc in each dc across, turn. Rep last row once more.
Row 4: 1ch, 1dc in each dc across, turn,

join into a ring with a sl st in first dc of row, taking care not to twist the rows – cont to work in rnds as follows:
Rnd 1: 1ch, 1dc in each of next 26dc around, join with a sl st in first dc of row (26 dc).
Rnd 2: 1dc in each of next 26dc.
Rep last rnd until the entire leg measures 11 cm (4¼ in), turn.
Now work in rows.

Leg shaping
Next row: 1ch, miss next dc, 1dc in each dc to end (marker), turn (25 dc).
Rep last row 8 times more (17 dc).
Next row: 1ch, 1dc in each dc across. Fasten off.
Make another leg in the same way.

Join legs
With WS out, join two legs at back and front gusset by working 1dc in each row-end edge from waist at centre front, down along centre front up along centre back to centre back waist. Turn out to RS.

Waistband
At waist edge, join in yarn A to a dc at centre back waist edge, work 1ch, 1dc in each dc around waist (34 dc).
Next rnd: 1dc in each dc around, sl st to first dc of rnd.
Fasten off.

TO FINISH

Weave in all ends. Thread the ribbon

through waistband, through first dc after centre front seam, then every 3rd dc around waistband.

Basic Shoes

FINISHED SIZE

8 cm (3¼ in) long

MATERIALS

- **RYC** *Cashsoft 4-ply*
  One ball of Dive 427
- Hook size: 3.50 mm (E-4)
- Two 5 mm (³⁄₁₆ in) buttons
- Blue thread for attaching buttons

TENSION

9 sts and 10 rows measured over 5 cm (2 in), working double crochet in MC and using 3.50 mm (E-4) hook.

SHOES

Make 2 alike.

Foundation row: Beg at toe, make 2ch.
Rnd 1: 6dc in 2nd ch from hook.
Rnd 2: 2dc in each of next 6dc (12 dc).
Rnd 3: *1dc in each of next 2dc, 2dc in next dc, rep from * around (16 dc).
Rnd 4: 1dc in each of next 16dc.
Rep last rnd twice more.
Shape top of shoe
Rnd 7: [Miss next dc, 1dc in next dc] 4 times, 1dc in each of next 8dc, turn (12 dc).

Now work in rows.
Shape upper
Row 1: 1ch, 1dc in each of next 6dc, turn.
Row 2: 1ch, 2dc in first dc, 1dc in each of next 3dc, 2dc in next dc, 1dc in last dc, turn (8 dc).
Row 3: 1ch, 2dc in first dc, 1dc in each of next 5dc, 2dc in next dc, 1dc in last dc, turn (10 dc).
Row 4: 1ch, 2dc in first dc, 1dc in each of next 7dc, 2dc in next dc, 1dc in last dc, turn (12 dc).
Row 5: 1ch, 1dc in each of next 12dc, turn.
Rep last row twice more.
Next rnd: 1dc in first dc of this row to join back of heel. Starting at heel, work 21dc evenly around upper edge of shoe, sl st in first dc of rnd.
Fasten off.
Sew up heel seam. Weave in ends.

SHOE STRAPS

Make 2 alike.

Foundation row: Make 10ch.
Row 1: 1dc in 2nd ch from hook, 1dc in each ch across (9 dc).
Fasten off, leaving tail ends long enough to sew strap to the shoe.

TO FINISH

Join one side of the strap to dc at upper shaping. Sew the other side of the strap in place with a button.

Basic Skirt

FINISHED SIZE

7 cm (2¾ in) long and 20 cm (7¾ in) in diameter around waist

MATERIALS

- **Debbie Bliss** *Cotton Denim Aran*
  One ball of Denim Blue 14503 (MC)
- Hook: 6.50 mm (K-10½)
- One 8 mm (⁵⁄₁₆ in) button
- Three 5 mm (³⁄₁₆ in) buttons for decoration (optional)
- Thread for attaching buttons

TENSION

7 sts and 6½ rows measured over 5 cm (2 in), working double crochet in MC and using 6.50 mm (K-10½) hook.

SKIRT

Foundation row: Beg at the waist edge, make 24ch, turn.
Row 1: 1dc in 2nd ch from hook, 1dc in each ch across, turn (23 dc).
Row 2: 1ch, 1dc in each dc across, do not twist yarn, join with sl st in 1ch to form a ring. Now work in rows.
Rnd 1: 1dc in each dc around (23 dc).
Rnd 2: 1dc in each of next 23dc.
Rep last rnd 5 times more, ending sl st in next dc.
Fasten off.

TO FINISH

At each side of the skirt at waist, pinch in 2dc to wrong side and catch them with a couple of stitches to create a dart. Sew a button at the back that is just large enough for a stitch to fasten over it and be secure.

Sew the three smaller buttons evenly down the front (optional).

Basic Hat

FINISHED SIZE

11 cm (4¼ in) in diameter

MATERIALS

- **RYC** *Cashsoft Aran*
  One ball of Bud 006 (MC)
- **Adriafil** *Angora Carezza*
  Small amount of Pink for brim (A)
- Hook: 5.00 mm (H-8)

TENSION

9 sts and 8 rnds measured over 5 cm (2 in), working double crochet in MC and using 5.00 mm (H-8) hook.

HAT

The crown and the brim are worked as one.

Foundation row: Beg at top of crown, using yarn MC, make 2ch.

Rnd 1: 6dc in 2nd ch from hook.

Rnd 2: 2dc in each of next 6dc (12 dc).
Rnd 3: *1dc in next dc, 2dc in next dc, rep from * around (18 dc).
Rnd 4: *1dc in each of next 2dc, 2dc in next dc, rep from * around (24 dc).
Rnd 5: *1dc in each of next 3dc, 2dc in next dc, rep from * around (30 dc).
Rnd 6: *1dc in each of next 4dc, 2dc in next dc, rep from * around (36 dc).

Shape sides
Rnd 7: 1tr in each of next 36dc.
Rnd 8: 1tr in each of next 36tr.
Fasten off yarn MC with sl st in next tr. Weave in end.

Brim
Join in yarn A with sl st in sl st of last rnd.

Rnd 9: *Miss next tr, 1tr in each of next 3tr, rep from * around (27 tr).
Rnd 10: [Miss next tr, 1tr in each of next 3tr] 6 times, miss next tr, 1 tr in each of last 2tr (20 tr).
Fasten off. Pull up centre loose end to close the ring, weave in ends, leaving a short loop at centre of hat.

Sun Clothes

Let's go surfin'! Our toys love adventure and always get out when the sun is bright. A striped one-piece makes ideal sunbathing attire; a swimming cap and flip-flops are stylish beach accessories.

Swimsuit

FINISHED SIZE
To fit Basic Doll or Bear (pages 10 and 13)

MATERIALS
- **Debbie Bliss** *Cashmerino Aran*
  Half a ball of Pink 006 (MC)
- **RYC** *Cashsoft 4-ply*
  Small amount of Dive 427 (A)
- Hook: 5.00 mm (H-8)
- Three 5 mm (³/₁₆ in) buttons for decoration (optional)
- Thread for attaching buttons

TENSION
9 sts and 10 rnds measured over 5 cm (2 in), working double crochet in MC and using 5.00 mm (H-8) hook.

NOTE:
Before beg the second rnd in each section, place a marker or short length of contrasting yarn across your crochet and

up against the loop on the hook and above the working yarn. Work Rnd 2 then slip the marker out and place it at the beg of the next rnd and so on. The marker will indicate where each subsequent rnd starts.

SWIMSUIT FRONT & BACK
Foundation rnd: Beg at the top of the costume, using MC, make 22ch, taking care not to twist the chain join with a sl st in first ch to form ring.
Rnd 1: 1dc in each ch around (22 dc).

Rnd 2: 1dc in each dc around.
Rep last rnd twice more, fasten off yarn MC with sl st in next dc.
Rnd 5: Join in yarn A with sl st in same place as sl st of last rnd was worked, 1dc in each dc around.
Rnd 6: 1dc in each dc around.
Rep last rnd twice more, fasten off yarn A with sl st in next dc.
Join in yarn MC as rnd 5, then rep last 4 rnds in yarn MC once more, fasten off yarn MC with sl st in next dc.

Rnd 13: Join in yarn A with sl st in same place as sl st of last rnd was worked, 1dc in each of next 22dc, turn.

Now work in rows.

Shape front legs

Row 1: 1ch, 1dc in each of next 9dc, place marker, turn (9 dc).

Row 2: Sl st in first dc, 1ch, 1dc in each of next 7dc, miss last dc, turn (7 dc).

Row 3: Sl st in first dc, 1ch, 1dc in each of next 5dc, miss last dc, turn (5 dc).

Row 4: Sl st in first dc, 1ch, 1dc in each of next 3dc, miss last dc, turn (3 dc).

Row 5: 1ch, 1dc in each dc of next 3dc, turn.

Rep last row once more.

Fasten off.

Shape back legs

Row 1: At marker join in yarn A with sl st in next dc, 1dc in each of next 13dc, turn (13 dc).

Row 2: Sl st in first dc, 1ch, 1dc in each of next 11dc, miss last dc, turn (11 dc).

Row 3: Sl st in first dc, 1ch, 1dc in each of next 9dc, miss last dc, turn (9 dc).

Row 4: Sl st in first dc, 1ch, 1dc in each of next 7dc, miss last dc, turn (7 dc).

Row 5: Sl st in first dc, 1ch, 1dc in each of next 7dc, miss last dc, turn (5 dc).

Row 6: Sl st in first dc, 1ch, 1dc in each of next 7dc, miss last dc, turn (3 dc).

Fasten off.

Sew up the gusset then work border.

Border

Join on yarn MC with sl st in any dc around leg. Work in dc evenly around each leg.

Fasten off. Weave in ends.

STRAPS

Make 2 alike.

Using yarn A, make 11ch.

Row 1: 1dc in 2nd ch from hook, 1dc in each ch across (10 dc).

Fasten off. Weave in ends.

TO FINISH

At upper edge roll down the top to RS for 3 rows. Sew each strap to the inside of the costume behind the rolled over part – you can dress the doll/bear in the swimsuit first to get the straps into position correctly before sewing in place. Sew buttons onto front of swimsuit.

Swimming Cap

FINISHED SIZE

To fit Basic Doll or Bear (pages 10 and 13)

MATERIALS

- **Sirdar** *Bonus Chunky*
  Small amount of Bright Orange (MC)
- **Opal** *Uni 4-ply*
  Small amount of Grass Green for flowers (A) (optional)
- Hook: 5.00 mm (H-8)
- One button
- Yarn needle

TENSION

9 sts and 10 rnds measured over 5 cm (2 in), working double crochet in MC and using 5.00 mm (H-8) hook.

CAP

Foundation row: Beg at top of crown, using yarn MC, make 2ch.

Rnd 1: 6dc in 2nd ch from hook.

Rnd 2: 2dc in each of next 6dc (12 dc).

Rnd 3: *1dc in next dc, 2dc in next dc, rep from * around (18 dc).

Rnd 4: *1dc in each of next 2dc, 2dc in next dc, rep from * around (24 dc).

Rnd 5: *1dc in each of next 3dc, 2dc in next dc, rep from * around (30 dc).

Rnd 6: *1dc in each of next 4dc, 2dc in

next dc, rep from * around (36 dc).

Shape sides

NOTE: *For bear's hat only, follow next two rnds to make gaps in side for ears – for dolls go straight to Rnd 9.*

Rnd 7: Miss first 5dc, make 5ch, 1dc in each of next 13dc, miss next 5dc, make 5ch, 1dc in each of next 13dc (36 sts).

Rnd 8: [1dc in each of next 5ch, 1dc in each of next 13dc] twice (36 dc).

Rnd 9: 1dc in each of next 36 dc.

Rep last rnd twice more for bear's hat and 4 times more for doll's hat.

Next rnd: *Miss next dc, 1dc in each of next 3dc, rep from * around (27 dc).

Next rnd: 1dc in each of next 27dc.

Rep last rnd twice more.

Fasten off. Weave in ends.

FIRST CHINSTRAP

Using yarn MC, make 7ch.

Row 1: 1dc in 2nd ch from hook, 1dc in each ch across (6 dc).

Fasten off.

SECOND CHINSTRAP

Using yarn MC, make 9ch.

Row 1: 1dc in 2nd ch from hook, miss next ch, make 1ch (to make buttonhole), 1 dc in each of next 6ch.

Fasten off.

FLORAL ADORNMENTS (OPTIONAL)

Using yarn A, make 4ch, sl st in first ch to form ring.

Rnd 1: 1ch, 7dc into ring, sl st in first ch of this rnd.

Rnd 2: [3ch, 3tr tog all in back loop of next dc, 3ch, 1dc into centre ring, miss next dc] 4 times.

Fasten off.

Make as many or as few as you wish.

TO FINISH

Hand-sew a chin strap to each side of the hat. Hand-sew a button on the first chin strap near the end not attached to the hat. Hand-sew the flowers all over the hat.

Flip-Flops

FINISHED SIZE

To fit Basic Doll or Bear (pages 10 and 13)

MATERIALS

- **Opal *Uni 4-ply***
  Small amount of Grass Green (MC)
  Small amount of contrast colour for toe bar (A)
- Hook: 5.00 mm (H-8)
- Yarn needle

TENSION

9 sts and 10 rnds measured over 5 cm

(2 in), working double crochet in MC and using 5.00 mm (H-8) hook.

SOLES

Make 2 alike.

Foundation row: Using MC, make 2ch.

Rnd 1: 4dc in 2nd ch from hook.

Rnd 2: *1dc in next ch, 2dc in next, rep from * once more (6dc).

Rnd 3: *1dc in next dc, 2dc in next, rep from * around (9dc).

Rnd 4: 1dc in each of next dc.

Rep last rnd three times more.

Shape the heel

Flatten the sole down so that the last stitch ends at the side of the shoe, work 1ch, then work 1dc across both thicknesses into each of next 4dc, turn.

Next row: 1ch, 1dc in each of next 4dc, turn.

Rep last row three times more, (or until the sole fits the length of your doll's/bear's foot).

Fasten off. Weave in ends.

TOE BARS

Make 2 alike.

Using yarn A, make 16ch. Fasten off.

TO FINISH

Sew each loose end of the toe bar to halfway along the sole; join the centre ch to the toe end.

Hula Hula Lula

Aloha! With her grass skirt and flowery lei, this Hawaiian doll brings a touch of paradise to any child's room. Sporting a red headband, a yellow orchid behind her ear and bangles, Lula loves to accessorize in colour.

Doll

FINISHED SIZE
42 cm (16½ in) tall × 50 cm (19¾ in) wide (arms outstretched)

MATERIALS
- **Rooster *Almerino DK***
  One ball of Hazelnut 202 (MC)
- **Twilleys *Freedom Cotton DK***
  One ball of Cotton Black for hair (A)
- Hook: 3.50 mm (H-8)
- Small pieces of felt for eyes
- Black thread for sewing on eyes
- Two 6 mm (¼ in) black glass beads or similar for eyes
- Pink embroidery thread for mouth
- Polyester toy fibrefill or wadding
- Yarn needle

TENSION
9 sts and 9 rows measured over 5 cm (2 in) working double crochet in MC and using 5.00 mm (E-4) hook.

HEAD, BODY, ARMS, FEET, & LEGS
Using yarn MC and 3.50 mm (E-4) hook, make the same as for Basic Doll (page 13).

Wardrobe

MATERIALS
- **Sirdar *Snuggly DK***
  Small amount of Lilac 0219 (A)
- **GGH *Big Easy***
  Small amount of Turquoise 021 (B)
- **Lobster Pot *Bulky***
  Small amount of New Seagrass (C)
- **RYC *Cashcotton 4-ply***
  Small amount of Sugar 901 (D)
- **Jaeger *Baby Merino 4-ply***
  Small amount of Snowdrop 0102 (E)
- **Anchor *Tapisserie Wool*** various shades – small amounts needed
- Hook size: 4.00 mm (G-6)
- Three 5 mm (³⁄₁₆ in) buttons for decoration (optional)
- Thread for attaching button

TENSION
12 sts and 10 rows measured over 5 cm (2 in), working double crochet in yarn A and using 4.00 mm (G-6) hook.

TANKINI BOTTOM
Using yarn A and 4.00 mm (G-6) hook, make as Tankini Bottom (page 15).

TANKINI TOP
Foundation row: Using yarn D and 4.00 mm (G-6) hook, make 40ch.
Row 2: 1tr in 4th ch from hook, 1tr in each ch across, join with sl st in top of 3ch at beg of row to form ring, taking care not to twist the row (38 tr). Fasten off.
Rnd 1: Join in yarn E with sl st in last tr, 1dc in each tr around.
Rnd 2: 1dc in each dc around.
Rep last rnd once more.
Fasten off.

GRASS SKIRT
Foundation row: Using yarn B and 4.00 mm (G-6) hook, make 27ch.
Row 1: 1dc in 2nd ch from hook, 1dc in each ch across, turn (26 dc).
Row 2: 2ch (counts as 1ch and 1dc), miss first dc to make buttonhole – 1dc in each dc to end.
Fasten off.
Sew on button at front.
To join 'grass', cut 28 cm (11 in) lengths of yarn C. Taking one length at a time, bend in half and, using a crochet hook, pull the loop through a dc stitch along the foundation row of the skirt

waistband. Pass the cut ends through the loops, then pull the cut ends firmly so that the knot lies close to the dc stitch. Continue with this fringing technique along the band.

LEI

Foundation row: Using any colour for flower and 4.00 mm (G-6) hook, make 7ch, join with sl st to form ring.
Rnd 1: Working over the tail end, 14dc into ring, sl st in first dc of rnd.
Rnd 2: 4ch, (4dtr tog, inserting hook twice in next dc and twice in foll dc, 3ch, 1dc in next dc, 3ch) 4 times, 4dtr tog inserting hook as before, 3ch, sl st in first ch of rnd.
Fasten off. Draw up the centre hole a little, leaving a tiny hole for threading. Weave in all ends.
Make as many flowers as you want for the lei and thread onto a single length of yarn.

HEADBAND

Foundation row: Using yarn E and 4.00 mm (G-6) hook, make 38ch.
Row 1: 1dc in 2nd ch from hook, 1dc in each ch across (37 dc).
Fasten off.
Sew up the row-end edges to join into a band. Weave in the ends.

SANDALS

Make 2 alike.
Sole
Foundation row: Using Tapisserie Wool and 4.00 mm (G-6) hook, make 13 ch.
Row 1: 1dc in 2nd ch from hook, 1dc in each ch across, turn (12 dc).
Row 2: 1ch, 1dc in each dc across, turn.
Rep last row 7 times more.
Fasten off.
Fold into 3 layers across foundation and finishing rows, sew up to hold in place.

Upper strap
Foundation row: Using Tapisserie Wool and 4.00 mm (G-6) hook, make 9ch.
Row 1: 1dc in 2nd ch from hook, 1dc in each ch across, turn (8 dc).
Row 2: 1ch, 1dc in each dc across.
Fasten off.
Sew to each side of the sole (a little more to the front than the back).

Sailor Bear

Ships ahoy! This little fella's had more than his fair share of excitement on the high seas. With his smart hat and tie, he's an invaluable treasure!

Sailor Bear

FINISHED SIZE
31 cm (12¼ in) tall × 35 cm (13¾ in) wide (arms outstretched)

MATERIALS
- **Brown Sheep Company** *Lambs Pride Worsted*
  One ball of Cream M–10 (MC)
- Hook: 5.00 mm (H-8)
- Black embroidery thread for attaching beads and for mouth
- 30 cm (12 in) dark grey DK yarn for nose
- Two 6 mm (¼ in) black glass beads or similar for eyes
- Polyester toy fibrefill or wadding
- Yarn needle

TENSION
9 sts and 8 rnds measured over 5 cm (2 in), working double crochet in MC and using 5.00 mm (H-8) hook.

NOTE:

Before beg the second rnd in each section, place a marker or short length of contrasting yarn across your crochet and up against the loop on the hook and above the working yarn. Work Rnd 2 then slip the marker out and place it at the beg of the next rnd and so on. The marker will indicate where each subsequent rnd starts.

HEAD, BODY, ARMS, & LEGS

Make as for Basic Bear (page 10) then make up in the same way.

Sailor's Trousers

FINISHED SIZE

17 cm (6¾ in) long and 23 cm (9 in) in diameter around waist

MATERIALS

- **Santos *Denim***
  One ball of Denim (MC)
- **Jaeger *Roma***
  One ball of Snow White 001 (A)
- Hook: 5.00 mm (H-8)

TROUSERS

Make as for Basic Trousers (see page 18) without following the colour sequence used to create stripes. Use the following colour sequence instead:

Foundation row and Row 1 – yarn MC.
Row 2 onwards – yarn A.
Continue in yarn A until you reach the waistband – change to yarn MC.

Sailor's Top

FINISHED SIZE

11 cm (4¼ in) long × 15 cm (6 in) wide

MATERIALS

- **Santos *Denim***
  One ball of Denim (MC)
- **Jaeger *Roma***
  One ball of Snow White 001 (A)
- Small amount of dark grey DK yarn for tie (B)
- Hook: 5.00 mm (H-8)
- Yarn needle

TENSION

8 sts and 9 rows measured over 5 cm (2 in), working double crochet in MC and using 5.00 mm (H-8) hook.

FRONT

Foundation row: Using yarn A, beg at front waist edge, make 18ch.

Row 1 (RS): 1tr in 4th ch from hook, 1tr in each ch across, turn (16 tr).

Row 2: 3ch (counts as first tr), miss first tr, 1 tr in each tr across, turn.

Row 3: Join in yarn MC, 1ch, 1dc in each tr across, turn (16 dc).

Row 4: 1ch, 1dc in each dc across.** Rep last row 10 times more.

Shape left front 'V'

Row 15: 1ch, 1dc in each of next 8dc, turn (8 dc).

Row 16: Sl st in first dc, 1ch, 1dc in each of next 7dc, turn (7 dc).

Row 17: 1ch, 1dc in each of next 5dc, miss next dc, 1dc in next dc, turn (6 dc).

Row 18: Sl st in first dc, 1ch, 1dc in each of next 5dc, turn (5 dc).

Row 19: 1ch, 1dc in each of next 3dc, miss next dc, 1dc in next dc, turn (4 dc).

Row 20: Sl st in first dc, 1ch, 1dc in each of next 3dc (3 dc).

Row 21: 1ch, 1dc in each of next 3dc. Fasten off.

Shape right front 'V'

Row 15: With RS facing, join in yarn MC to centre front, counting in 8dc from side edge, 1ch, 1dc in each of next 8dc, turn (8 dc).

Row 16: 1ch, 1dc in each of next 6dc, miss next dc, 1dc in next dc, turn (7 dc).

Row 17: Sl st in first dc, 1ch, 1dc in each of next 6dc, turn (6 dc).

Row 18: 1ch, 1dc in each of next 4dc, miss next dc, 1dc in next dc, turn (5 dc).

Row 19: Sl st in first dc, 1ch, 1dc in each of next 4dc, turn (4 dc).

Row 20: 1ch, 1dc in each of next 2dc, miss next dc, 1dc in next dc, turn (3 dc).

Row 21: 1ch, 1dc in each of next 3dc. Fasten off.

BACK

Work as for front up to **. Rep last row 15 times more.

Shape back neck

Next row (WS): 1ch, 1dc in each of next 5dc, turn.

Next row: Sl st in first dc, 1ch, miss next dc, 1dc in each of next 3dc (3 dc). Fasten off.

Next row: With WS facing, miss centre 6dc, join in yarn MC to next dc, 1ch, 1dc in same dc, 1dc in each of next 4dc, turn (5 dc).

Next row: 1ch, 1dc in each of next 2dc, miss next dc, 1dc in next dc (3 dc). Fasten off.

Using backstitch, sew up the shoulder seams and up from waist edge 6 cm (2½ in) at each side.

SLEEVES

Make 2 alike.

With RS facing, join in yarn MC in shoulder seam at armhole edge, 1ch, work 23dc evenly around armhole. Place marker, cont working in rnds until sleeve measures 2.5 cm (1 in), ending with sl st in first dc of previous rnd. Fasten off. Weave in ends.

TO FINISH

Weave in all ends.

With RS facing, join in yarn A at lower point of front 'V', work in dc evenly around neck edge, sl st to first dc. Fasten off.

BOW FOR SHIRT FRONT

Foundation row: Using yarn B, make 19ch.

Row 1: 1dc in 2nd ch from hook, 1dc in each ch across (18 dc). Fasten off. Weave in ends, twist a loop, sew to front of shirt.

Sailor's Shoes

FINISHED SIZE

7 cm (2¾ in) × 4 cm (1½ in)

MATERIALS

- **RYC *Cashsoft DK***
  Small amount of Thunder 518 (MC)
- Hook: 5.00 mm (H-8)
- Yarn needle

TENSION

8 sts and 9 rows measured over 5 cm
(2 in), working double crochet in MC and
using 5.00 mm (H-8) hook.

SHOES

Make 2 alike.

Foundation row: Beg at toe, using yarn
MC, make 2ch.

Rnd 1: 6dc in 2nd ch from hook.

Rnd 2: 2dc in each of next 6dc (12 dc).

Rnd 3: 2dc in each of next 12dc (24 dc).

Rnd 4: 1dc in each of next 24dc.

Rep last rnd 4 times more.

Shape top of shoe

Rnd 9: 1ch, (miss next dc, sl st in next dc)
6 times, 1dc in each of next 12dc, turn
(18 sts).

Now work in rows.

Shape sides

Next row: 1ch, 1dc in each of next 12dc,
turn.

Rep last row 4 times more.

Fasten off. Sew up the heel seam.

Top of shoe

Join in yarn MC at heel seam, 2ch, work
in htr evenly around top edge of shoe,

sl st in top of 2ch.
Fasten off. Weave in ends.

Sailor's Cap

FINISHED SIZE

17 cm (6¾ in) in diameter

MATERIALS

- **Jaeger *Roma***
  Small amount of Snow White 001 (A)
- **RYC *Cashsoft DK***
  Small amount of Thunder 518 (B)
- **Anchor *Tapisserie Wool***
  Small amount of Cherry 8216 for
  hat tassel (C)
- Hook: 5.00 mm (H-8)

TENSION

8 sts and 9 rows measured over 5 cm
(2 in), working double crochet in MC and
using 5.00 mm (H-8) hook.

CAP

Foundation row: Beg at top, using yarn
A, make 2ch.

Rnd 1: 8dc in 2nd ch from hook.

Rnd 2: *1dc in next dc, 2dc in next dc,
rep from * around (12 dc).

Rnd 3: *1dc in each of next 2dc, 2dc in
next dc, rep from * around (16 dc).

Rnd 4: *1dc in each of next 3dc, 2dc in
next dc, rep from * around (20 dc).

Rnd 5: *1dc in each of next 4dc, 2dc in
next dc, rep from * around (24 dc).

Rnd 6: *1dc in each of next 5dc, 2dc in
next dc, rep from * around (28 dc).

Rnd 7: *1dc in each of next 6dc, 2dc in
next dc, rep from * around (32 dc).

Rnd 8: 1dc in each of next 32dc.

Rep last rnd twice more.

Rnd 11: *1dc in next dc, miss next dc, rep
from * around (16 dc).

Fasten off.

Rnd 12: Join in yarn B with sl st in last dc,
1ch, 1dc in each of next 16 dc.

Rep last rnd once more. Fasten off.

Rnd 14: Join in yarn MC with sl st in last
dc, 1ch, 1dc in each of next 16dc.

Fasten off. Weave in ends.

TO FINISH

To make the tassel, cut short lengths of
red Tapisserie Wool, bend in half, and
hook the loop through any dc at the top
of the cap. Pass the raw ends through
the loop, and pull through the loop to
lie flat against the cap. Bunch up the
strands, then tie them around the
middle with another length of Tapisserie
Wool. Trim if necessary. Sew the cap to
the bear's head.

Princess Peony

This golden-haired princess will surely win the heart of any little girl. Pretty in pink, she makes an enchanting best friend for her proud owner.

Doll

FINISHED SIZE
42 cm (16½ in) tall × 50 cm (19¾ in) wide (arms outstretched)

MATERIALS
- **Jaeger *Aqua Cotton***
  One ball of Talc 302 (MC)
- **Debbie Bliss *Cashmerino Astrakhan***
  One ball of Gold 0707 for hair (A)
- Hook: 3.50 mm (E-4)
- Small pieces of felt for eyes
- Black thread for sewing on eyes
- Two 6 mm (¼ in) black glass beads or similar for eyes
- Pink embroidery thread for sewing mouth
- Polyester toy fibrefill or wadding
- Yarn needle

TENSION
As for Basic Doll (see page 13).

NOTE:

Before beg the second rnd in each section, place a marker or short length of contrasting yarn across your crochet and up against the loop on the hook and above the working yarn. Work Rnd 2, then slip the marker out and place it at the beg of the next rnd and so on. The marker will indicate where each subsequent rnd starts.

HEAD, BODY, ARMS, FEET & LEGS

Using yarn MC and 3.50 mm (E-4) hook, make the same as for Basic Doll (see page 13).

Wardrobe

FINISHED SIZE

Gown: 23 cm (9 in) long

MATERIALS

- **Debbie Bliss** *Baby Cashmerino*
  Two balls of Pink 006 (MC)
- **RYC** *Cashsoft 4-ply*
  One ball of Rose Lake 421 (A)
- **RYC** *Cashcotton 4-ply*
  Small amount of Cyclamen 00911 (B)
- **Karabella Yarns** *Vintage Mercerized Cotton*
  Small amount of Gold 320 (C)
- Hook: 3.50 mm (E-4) and 4.00 mm (G-6)

- Two short lengths of ribbon for top of the hat
- Yarn needle

TENSION

7 sts and 4½ rnds measured over 5 cm (2 in), working half treble crochet in MC and using 4.00 mm (G-6) hook.

GOWN

Foundation row: Beg with bodice, using yarn MC and 4.00 mm (G-6) hook, make 32ch.

Row 1: 1htr in 2nd ch from hook, 1htr in each ch across, join with sl st in first htr to form ring and cont to work in rnds (31 htr).

Rnd 1: 1htr in each of next 31htr.

Rnd 2: 1htr in each of next 31htr.

Rep last rnd 3 times more, ending with sl st in first htr of rnd. Fasten off yarn MC.

Shape skirt

Rnd 6: Join in yarn A to same place as sl st was worked, 1dc in each of next 15htr, 3dc in next htr, 1dc in each of next 15htr (33 dc).

Rnd 7: 1dc in each of next 15dc, 2dc in next dc, 1dc in each of next 3dc, 2dc in next dc, 1dc in each of next 13dc (35 dc).

Rnd 8: 1dc in each of next 15dc, 2dc in next dc, 1dc in each of next 5dc, 2dc in next dc, 1dc in each of next 13dc (37 dc).

Rnd 9: 1dc in each of next 15dc, 2dc in

next dc, 1dc in each of next 7dc, 2dc in next dc, 1dc in each of next 13dc (39 dc).

Rnd 10: 1dc in each of next 15dc, 2dc in next dc, 1dc in each of next 9dc, 2dc in next dc, 1dc in each of next 13dc (41 dc). Cont increasing at centre front until there are 61dc, with 27dc after first increase.

Rnd 20: 1dc in each of next 61dc. Rep last rnd until gown measures 23 cm (9 in) from top of bodice. Fasten off.

For the heart motif, make 22ch using yarn C (slipper colour) and 3.50 mm (E-4) hook. Fasten off and twist into a heart shape onto the front of the bodice, securing with a few stitches.

RUFFLE

Foundation row: Using yarn B and 3.50 mm (E-4) hook, make 34ch.

Row 1: 1dc in 2nd ch from hook, 1 dc in each ch across, turn (33 dc).

Row 2: 1ch, 1dc in each dc across, turn (33 dc).

Row 3: 1ch, 1dc in first dc, *miss 1dc, 5tr in next dc, miss 1dc, 1dc in next dc, rep from * to end.
Fasten off.

TO FINISH

Sew the middle three 'scallops' of the ruffle onto the centre front of the bodice at the foundation row. Join the two ruffle ends, then sew the seam onto the back of the bodice.

PRINCESS HAT

Foundation row: Beg at the pointed top, using yarn B and 4.00 mm (G-6) hook, make 2ch.
Rnd 1: 6dc in 2nd ch from hook.
Rnd 2: 1dc in each of next 6dc (6 dc).
Rnd 3: [1dc in next dc, 2dc in next dc] 3 times (9 dc).
Rnd 4: 1dc in each of next 9dc.
Rnd 5: [1dc in each of next 2dc, 2dc in next dc] 3 times (12 dc).
Rnd 6: 1dc in each of next 12dc.
Rnd 7: [1dc in each of next 3dc, 2dc in next dc] 3 times (15 dc).
Rnd 8: 1dc in each of next 15dc.
Rnd 9: [1dc in each of next 4dc, 2dc in next dc] 3 times (18 dc).
Rnd 10: 1dc in each of next 18dc.
Rnd 11: [1dc in each of next 5dc, 2dc in next dc] 3 times (21 dc).
Rnd 12: [1dc in each of next 6dc, 2dc in next dc] 3 times (24 dc).
Rnd 13: [1dc in each of next 7dc, 2dc in next dc] 3 times (27 dc).
Rnd 14: 1dc in each of next 27dc.
Rnd 15: [1dc in each of next 8dc, 2dc in next dc] 3 times (30 dc).
Rnd 16: 1dc in each of next 30dc.
Rnd 17: [1dc in each of next 9dc, 2dc in next dc] 3 times (33 dc).
Rnd 18: 1dc in each of next 33dc, ending with sl st in top of first dc of rnd. Fasten off.
Join in yarn MC to place where sl st was worked.
Rnd 19: 1htr in each dc around, ending with sl st in top of first htr of rnd. Fasten off. Weave in ends. Sew two short lengths of coordinating ribbon to the top of the hat and tie in a bow.
For the chinstraps, using yarn B, make 2 lengths of 23ch, fasten off and sew to the insides of each side of the hat. Weave in ends.

BELT

Foundation row: Using yarn C and 3.50 mm (E-4) hook, make 42ch.
Row 1: 1dc in 2nd ch from hook, 1dc in each ch across, turn (41 dc).
Row 2: *3ch, sl st in first of these 3ch, miss next dc, 1dc in next dc, repeat from * 16 times more, leaving rem 7dc unworked.
Fasten off.
The remaining few dc are used as the belt end. Tuck this into the first 3ch when belt is placed around waist. Weave in ends.

SLIPPERS

Foundation row: Beg at toe, using yarn C and 3.50 mm (E-4) hook, make 2ch.
Rnd 1: 6dc in 2nd ch from hook.
Rnd 2: 2dc in each of next 6dc (12 dc).
Rnd 3: *1dc in each of next 2dc, 2dc in next dc, rep from * around (16 dc).
Rnd 4: 1dc in each dc around (16 dc).
Rep last rnd twice more.
Shape top of slipper
Rnd 7: (Miss next dc, 1dc in next dc) 4 times, 1dc in each of next 8dc, turn (12 dc).
Shape sides
Now work in rows.
Row 1: 1ch, 1dc in each of next 6dc, turn.
Row 2: 1ch, 2dc in next dc, 1dc in each of next 3dc, 2dc in next dc, 1dc in next dc, turn (8 dc).
Row 3: 1ch, 2dc in next dc, 1dc in each of next 5dc, 2dc in next dc, 1dc in next dc, turn (10 dc).
Row 4: 1ch, 2dc in next dc, 1dc in each of next 7dc, 2dc in next dc, 1dc in next dc, turn (12 dc).
Row 5: 1ch, 1dc in each of next 12dc, turn.
Rep last row twice more.
Fasten off. Sew up the heel seam.
Ankle straps
Make 2 alike.
Make 20ch, fasten off. Weave in ends. Join the centre of the strap to the heel seam. Tie straps onto foot.

Molly the Mermaid

Elegant and serene, Molly's flowing locks and beautiful blue eyes make her a sight to behold at sea or on land. Join her in her underwater palace and watch the hours float by.

Mermaid

FINISHED SIZE
41 cm (16 in) tall × 50 cm (19 ¾ in) wide (arms outstretched)

MATERIALS
- **Jaeger** *Pure Cotton DK*
  One ball of Shell 0576 (MC)
- **Rowan** *All Seasons Cotton*
  One ball of Lime Leaf 217 for tail (A)
- **Sirdar** *Breeze*
  Small amount of Lime 068 for tail fins (B)
- **Anchor** *Tapisserie Wool*
  Small amount of 9096 and 9156 for tail ruffles in order of making (C)
- **Rowan** *4-ply Cotton*
  Small amount of 120 Orchid for shell in hair and for mouth (D)
- **Brown Sheep Company** *Cotton Fleece*
  One ball of Banana 620 for hair (E)
- Hook: 3.50 mm (E-4) and 2.50 mm (C-2)
- Small pieces of felt for eyes
- Black and pink embroidery thread for sewing on eyes and mouth detail
- Two 6 mm (¼ in) black glass beads or similar for eyes
- Polyester toy fibrefill or wadding
- Yarn needle

TENSION
12 sts and 12 rnds measured over 5 cm (2 in), working double crochet in MC and using 3.50 mm (E-4) hook.

NOTE:
Before beg the second rnd in each section, place a marker or short length of contrasting yarn across your crochet and up against the loop on the hook and above the working yarn. Work Rnd 2, then slip the marker out and place it at the beg of the next rnd and so on. The marker will indicate where each subsequent rnd starts.

HEAD, BODY, & ARMS
Using yarn MC and 3.50 mm (E-4) hook, make the same as for Basic Doll (page 13).

NOTE:
For the mermaid, make only the trunk of the Basic Doll.

TAIL
Foundation rnd: Using yarn A and 3.50 mm (E-4) hook, beg at tip of tail, make 3ch, join with a sl st to form ring.

Rnd 1: Working over tail end, 1dc in next ch, 2dc in next ch, 1dc in last ch (4 dc).

Rnd 2: 1dc in each of next 4dc.

Rnd 3: 2dc in each of next 4dc (8 dc).

Rnd 4: 1dc in each of next 8dc.

Rep last rnd once more.

Rnd 6: 1dc in next dc, 2dc in next dc, 1dc in each of next 3dc, 2dc in next dc, 1dc in each of next 2dc (10 dc).

Rnd 7: 1dc in each of next 10dc.

Rep last rnd once more.

Rnd 9: [1dc in each of next 2dc, 2dc in next dc] 3 times, 1dc in next dc (13 dc).

Rnd 10: 1dc in each of next 13dc.

Rep last rnd once more.

Rnd 12: [1dc in each of next 3dc, 2dc in next dc] 3 times, 1dc in next dc (16 dc).

Rnd 13: 1dc in each of next 16dc.

Rep last rnd once more.

Rnd 15: [1dc in each of next 7dc, 2dc in next dc] twice (18 dc).

Rnd 16: 1dc in each of next 18dc.

Rep last rnd once more.

Rnd 18: [1dc in each of next 8dc, 2dc in next dc] twice (20 dc).

Rnd 19: 1dc in each of next 20dc.

Rep last rnd once more.

Rnd 21: 1ch, 1dc in each of next 20dc, turn (21 sts).

Shell pattern

Row 1: 4ch, 3dtr in first dc, [miss 3dc, 1dc in next dc, miss 3dc, 7dtr in next dc] twice, miss 3dc, 1dc in 1ch at beg of previous row, turn.

Row 2: 4ch, 3dtr in first dc, [miss 3dtr, 1dc in next dtr (the centre dtr of 7), miss 3dtr, 7dtr in next dc] twice, miss 3dtr, 1dc in 4th of 4ch at beg of previous row, turn.

Rep last row 5 times more.

Fasten off.

TAIL RUFFLE

Make 4 ruffles – one in yarn A, one in yarn B and two in yarn C.

Foundation row: Using appropriate yarn and using 3.50 mm (E-4) hook, make 30ch.

Row 1: 1dc in 2nd ch from hook, 1dc in each ch across, turn (29 dc).

Row 2: 1ch, 1dc in each dc across (29 dc).

Row 3: 1ch, 1dc in first dc, *miss 1dc, 5tr in next dc, miss 1dc, 1dc in next dc, rep from * to end.

Fasten off.

TAIL FINS

Make 2 alike.

Foundation rnd: Using yarn B and 3.50 mm (E-4) hook, beg at tip of tail, make 4ch, join with a sl st to form ring.

Rnd 1: Working over tail end, [1dc in next ch, 2dc in next ch] twice (6 dc).

Rnd 2: 1dc in each of next 6dc.

Rnd 3: [1dc in next dc, 2dc in next dc] 3 times (9 dc).

Rnd 4: 1dc in each of next 9dc.

Rnd 5: [1dc in next dc, 2dc in next dc] 4 times, 1dc in next dc (13 dc).

Rnd 6: 1dc in each dc around.

Rnd 7: [1dc in next dc, 2dc in next dc] 6 times, 1dc in next dc (19 dc).

Rnd 8: 1 dc in each of next 19dc.

Rep last rnd 5 times more.

Rnd 14: [1dc in each of next 2dc, miss next dc] 6 times, 1dc in next dc (13 dc).

Rnd 15: 1dc in each of next 13dc.

Rnd 16: [1dc in next dc, miss next dc] 6 times, 1dc in next dc (7 dc).

Rnd 17: 1dc in each of next 7dc.

Rep last rnd once more.

Fasten off.

SHELL (IN HAIR)

Foundation row: Using yarn D and 2.50 mm (C-2) hook, make 6ch.

Row 1: 1dc in 2nd ch from hook, 1 dc in each ch across (5 dc).

Row 2: 1ch, 1dc in each dc across (5 dc).

Row 3: 1ch, 1dc in first dc, miss 1dc, 5tr in next dc, miss 1dc, 1dc in next dc.

Fasten off.

TO FINISH

Follow instructions for Basic Doll (page 13).

Sew the finishing row of the first tail ruffle to the top of the tail (the wavy edges should lie over the top of the tail). Sew up the tail along the back seam. Ease to fit the top of the tail to the bottom edge of the body, oversew in place. Sew on the other three ruffles so that they fall one-third of the way down the tail.

At the tip of the tail, oversew the two tail fins at either side of the tail.

To sew on hair, cut yarn E into lengths of 36 cm (14¼ in) and follow instructions for Basic Doll (page 13). Sew the hair shell in place at the side of the head.

Tankini

MATERIALS

- **RYC *Cashsoft DK***
  Small amount of Ballad Blue 508 (MC)
- **Sirdar *Breeze***
  Small amount of Wisteria 069 for ruffle (A)
- Hook: 3.50 mm (E-4)
- Yarn needle

BACK AND FRONT

Foundation row: Using yarn A, beg with

the ruffle, make 50ch.

Row 1: 1dc in 2nd ch from hook, 1dc in next ch, *3ch, miss 1ch, 1dc in each of next 3ch, rep from * to last 3ch, 3ch, miss 1ch, 1dc in each of last 2ch, turn.

Row 2: 1ch, 1dc in first dc, *miss 1dc, 5tr in next 3ch loop, miss 1dc, 1dc in next dc, rep from * to end, turn.

Row 3: 5ch, miss first dc and next tr, *1dc in each of next 3tr, 3ch, miss (1tr, 1dc and 1tr), rep from * to last 5tr group, 1dc in each of next 3tr, 2ch, miss 1tr, 1tr in last dc.

Fasten off.

With RS facing, join in yarn MC to corner of foundation row edge and work 34dc evenly across straight edge of ruffle, turn.

Next row: 1ch, 1dc in each of next 34dc, turn.

Rep last row once more.

Fasten off.

STRAPS

Make 2 alike.

In yarn MC, make 12ch.

Fasten off.

TO FINISH

Sew up the back seam, oversew the straps at the arm positions. Fit the top onto the mermaid for accurate positioning.

Mirror

MATERIALS

- **Opal** *Uni 4-ply*
  Small amount of Hot Pink 1413 for back and handle (MC)
- **Rowan** *Lurex Shimmer*
  Small amount of Pewter 333 for glass (A)
- Hook size: 2.50 mm (C-2)
- Yarn needle

MIRROR BACK

Foundation row: Using yarn MC, make 2ch.

**Rnd 1: 6dc in 2nd ch from hook, join with sl st to first dc to form ring (6 dc).

Rnd 2: 1dc in each of next 6dc.

Rnd 3: [1dc in next dc, 2dc in next dc] 3 times (9 dc).**

Rnd 4: 2dc in each of next 9dc, sl st in first dc of rnd (18 dc).

Handle

Make 10 ch.

Row 1: 1tr in 4th ch from hook, 1tr in each of next 4ch, 1htr in next ch, [1dc, 1ch, 1dc] in last ch.

Fasten off. Weave in ends to stabilize handle.

MIRROR GLASS

Foundation row: Using yarn A, make 2ch. Work as for Mirror Back from ** to **.

Fasten off.

Sew the glass to the mirror back. Sew the mirror handle to the mermaid's right hand.

Animal Kingdom

These projects come to life with a little imagination and make excellent presents for boys and girls of all ages! Join Larry the Lobster in his hunt for some freshwater fun, or drift off to sleep with Sir Waldorf Walrus on his afternoon nap – or maybe joining Jenna the Giraffe at her afternoon tea party is more your scene?

George the Shark

Don't let his beady eyes and powerful tail deceive you. With embroidered facial features, a floppy fin and a big, white belly, George is the cutest creature in the deep blue sea and a loving companion for your small fry.

Shark

FINISHED SIZE

34 cm (13½ in) long

MATERIALS

- RYC *Cashsoft Aran*
  One ball of Tornado 008 (MC)
- **Debbie Bliss** *Cashmerino Aran*
  One ball of Cream 300101 for belly (A)
- Hook: 6.50 mm (K-10½) and 5.00 mm (H-8)
- Thread for attaching beads
- Black DK (light worsted weight) yarn for mouth
- Two 6 mm (¼ in) black glass beads or similar for eyes
- Polyester toy fibrefill or wadding
- Yarn needle

TENSION

7 sts and 6½ rows measured over 5 cm (2 in), working in double crochet in yarn MC and using 6.50 mm (K-10½) hook.

NOTE:

Before beg the second rnd in each section, place a marker or short length of contrasting yarn across your crochet and up against the loop on the hook and above the working yarn. Work Rnd 2, then slip the marker out and place it at the beg of the next rnd and so on. The marker will indicate where each subsequent rnd starts.

BODY

Foundation row: Beg at the nose, in yarn MC and using 6.50 mm (K-10½) hook, make 2ch.
Rnd 1: 6d⸏⸏⸏
Rnd 2: 1d⸏
Rep last r⸏
Rnd 4: *1dc in next dc, 2dc⸏
rep from * around (9 dc).
Rnd 5: 1dc in each of next 9dc.
Rep last rnd once more.
Rnd 7: *1dc in each of next 2dc, 2dc in next dc, rep from * around (12 dc).
Rnd 8: 1dc in each of next 12dc.
Now work back section by cont to work in rows.
Row 1: 1ch, 1dc in each of next 10dc, turn.
Row 2: 2ch, 1dc in 2nd ch from hook, 1dc in each of next 9dc, 2dc in last dc, turn (12 dc).
Row 3: 1ch, 1dc in each of next 12dc across, turn.

Rep last row 7 times more.
Row 11: 2ch, 1dc in 2nd ch from hook, 1dc in each dc to last dc, 2dc in last dc, turn (14 dc).
Row 12: 1dc in each dc across, turn.
Rep last 2 rows twice more (18 dc).
Row 17: 1dc in each dc across, turn.
Rep last row 6 times more.
Row 24: Place marker here, sl st in first dc, 1ch, 1dc in each of next 15dc, miss next dc, 1dc in last dc, place marker here, turn (16 dc).
Row 25: Sl st in first dc, 1ch, 1dc in each of next 13dc, miss next dc, 1dc in last dc, turn (14 dc).
Row 26: 1ch, 1dc in each dc across, turn.
Rep last row once more.
Row 28: Sl st in first dc, 1ch, 1dc in each of next 11dc, miss next dc, 1dc in last dc, turn (12 dc).
Row 29: 1ch, 1dc in each dc across, turn.
Rep last row 4 times more.
Row 34: Sl st in first dc, 1ch, 1dc in each of next 9dc, miss next dc, 1dc in last dc, join with sl st in first sl st of row to form a ring (10 dc).
Shape tail
Rnd 1: 1dc in each of next 10dc around.
Rnd 2: [2dc in next dc, 1dc in each of next 4dc] twice (12 dc).

Rnd 3: [2dc in next dc, 1dc in each of next 5dc] twice (14 dc).

Rnd 4: [2dc in next dc, 1dc in each of next 6dc] twice (16 dc).

Rnd 5: [2dc in next dc, 1dc in each of next 7dc] twice (18 dc).

Rnd 6: 1dc in each dc around (18 dc).

Shape bottom of tail

Rnd 7: 1dc in each of next 3dc, place marker here, turn.

Now cont to work in rows to shape bottom of tail.

Row 1: 1ch, 1dc in each of next 6dc, turn.

Rep last row once more.

Row 3: Sl st in first dc, 1ch, 1dc in each of next 3dc, miss next dc, 1dc in last dc, turn (4 dc).

Row 4: 1ch, 1dc in each of next 4dc, turn.

Row 5: Sl st in first dc, 1ch, 1dc in next dc, miss next dc, 1dc in last dc (2 dc). Fasten off, leaving a tail end for sewing up with later.

Top tail

Join in yarn MC with sl st in dc at marker on Rnd 7 of 'Shape bottom of tail'.

Row 1: 1ch, 1dc in each of next 13dc, turn.

Rep last row twice more.

Row 4: Sl st in first dc, 1ch, 1dc in each of next 10dc, miss next dc, 1dc in last dc, turn (11 dc).

Row 5: Sl st in first dc, 1ch, 1dc in each of next 8dc, miss next dc, 1dc in last dc, turn (9 dc).

Row 6: Sl st in first dc, 1ch, 1dc in each of next 6dc, miss next dc, 1dc in last dc, turn (7 dc).

Row 7: Sl st in first dc, 1ch, 1dc in each of next 4dc, miss next dc, 1dc in last dc, turn (5 dc).

Row 8: Sl st in first dc, 1ch, 1dc in each of next 2dc, miss next dc, 1dc in last dc, turn (3 dc).

Row 9: Miss first 2 dc, sl st in last dc. Fasten off and weave in the loose end.

BELLY

Foundation row: Beg at the chin, in yarn A and using 6.50 mm (K-10½) hook, make 7ch.

Row 1: 1dc in 2nd ch from hook, 1dc in each ch across, turn (6 dc).

Row 2: 2ch, 1dc in 2nd ch from hook, 1dc in each dc to last dc, 2dc in last dc, turn (8 dc).

Rep last row twice more (12 dc).

Row 5: 1ch, 1dc in each dc across, turn.

Rep last row twice more.

Row 8: 2ch, 1dc in 2nd ch from hook, 1dc in each dc to last dc, 2dc in last dc, turn (14 dc).

Row 9: 1ch, 1dc in each dc across, turn.

Rep last row once more.

Row 11: Sl st in first dc, 1ch, 1dc in each of next 11dc, miss next dc, 1dc in last dc, turn (12 dc).

Row 12: 1ch, 1dc in each dc across, turn.

Rep last row once more.

Row 14: Sl st in first dc, 1ch, 1dc in each of next 9dc, miss next dc, 1dc in last dc, turn (10 dc).

Row 15: 1ch, 1dc in each dc across, turn. Rep last row once more.

Row 17: Sl st in first dc, 1ch, 1dc in each of next 7dc, miss next dc, 1dc in last dc, turn (8 dc).

Row 18: 1ch, 1dc in each dc across, turn. Rep last row once more.

Row 20: Sl st in first dc, 1ch, 1dc in each of next 5dc, miss next dc, 1dc in last dc, turn (6 dc).

Row 21: 1ch, 1dc in each dc across, turn.

Row 22: Sl st in first dc, 1ch, 1dc in each of next 3dc, miss next dc, 1dc in last dc, turn (4 dc).

Row 23: Sl st in first dc, 1ch, 1dc in next dc, miss next dc, 1dc in last dc, turn (2 dc).

Row 24: Miss first dc, sl st in last dc. Fasten off.

DORSAL FIN

Foundation row: Beg at the pointed top, in yarn MC and using 5.00 mm (H-8) hook, make 2ch.

Rnd 1: 4dc in 2nd ch from hook.

Rnd 2: 1dc in each of next 4dc.

Rnd 3: 1dc in each of next 3dc, 2dc in next dc (5 dc).

Rnd 4: 1dc in each of next 4dc, 2dc in next dc (6 dc).

Rnd 5: 1dc in each of next 5dc, 2dc in next dc (7 dc).

Rnd 6: 1dc in each of next 6dc, 2dc in next dc (8 dc).

Rnd 7: 1dc in each of next 7dc, 2dc in next dc (9 dc).

Cont increasing 1dc on last dc of rnd for 4 more rnds (13 dc).

Fasten off, leaving a tail end for sewing to body later.

UPPER TAIL FIN

Foundation row: Beg at the pointed top, in yarn MC and using 5.00 mm (H-8) hook, make 2ch.

Rnd 1: 4dc in 2nd ch from hook.

Rnd 2: 1dc in each of next 4dc.

Rnd 3: 1dc in each of next 3dc, 2dc in next dc (5 dc).

Rnd 4: 1dc in each of next 4dc, 2dc in next dc (6 dc).

Rnd 5: 1dc in each of next 5dc, 2dc in next dc (7 dc).

Fasten off, leaving a tail end for sewing up to the body later.

LOWER TAIL FIN

Foundation row: Beg at the pointed top, in yarn MC and using 5.00 mm (H-8) hook, make 2ch.

Rnd 1: 4dc in 2nd ch from hook.

Rnd 2: 1dc in each of next 4dc.

Rnd 3: 1dc in each of next 3dc, 2dc in next dc (5 dc).

Rnd 4: 1dc in each of next 4dc, 2dc in next dc (6 dc).

Rnd 5: 1dc in each of next 5dc, 2dc in next dc (7 dc).

Rnd 6: 1dc in each of next 6dc, 2dc in next dc (8 dc).

Rnd 7: 1dc in each of next 7dc, 2dc in next dc (9 dc).

Fasten off, leaving a tail end for sewing up to the body later.

FRONT FINS

Make 4 – 2 using yarn MC and 2 using yarn A.

Foundation row: Using 6.50 mm (K-10½) hook, beg at the end which is sewn to the body, make 5ch.

Row 1: 1dc in 2nd ch from hook, 1dc in each of next 2ch, 2dc in last ch, turn (5 dc).

Row 2: 2ch, 1dc in 2nd ch from hook, 1dc in each dc across, turn (6 dc).

Row 3: 1ch, 1dc in each dc to last dc, 2dc in last dc, turn (7 dc).

Row 4: Sl st in first dc, 1ch, 1dc in each dc across, turn (6 dc).

Row 5: 1ch, 1dc in each dc across to last 2dc, miss next dc, 1dc in last dc, turn (5 dc).

Rep last 2 rows once more (3 dc).

Row 8: Miss first 2 dc, sl st in last dc, turn, make 1ch, and work in dc evenly all around the edge of the fin, sl st to first dc.

Fasten off and weave in the end.

TO FINISH

With RS facing and working backstitch, sew up bottom tail fin along the decreases, sew up the top tail fin.

Sew the belly to the chin and along the body to first markers, leaving a gap for turning through and stuffing. Stuff and close the gap. Turn RS out.

Mould the tail fins into a point with your fingers, weave in the ends at the pointed ends, use the other ends to sew the larger fin under the body just before the tail begins and the upper fin to the top of the body just before the tail.

Sew the dorsal fin halfway along the body to the upper edge. Weave in the end at the point and shape if necessary. Sew up the underbody, up to the first set of markers.

Make two sets of front fins by sewing one fin in MC to one fin in yarn A around the edges. Sew front fins to sides of body where body meets belly, referring to photograph for positioning.

Sew on two beads for eyes, 5 cm (2 in) from point of nose and spaced 5 cm (2 in) apart. Sew a mouth using the the black yarn, curving the mouth around the nose where the body meets the belly, starting and ending in line with the eyes and working a row of stem stitch.

Kangaroo Bag with Joey

Fill your 'roo's stomach with supplies from the outback! Totally practical, yet fun and huggable, this double-crocheted carryall has a drawstring closure, durable straps (shaped as the ears), and ample space for all your young one's belongings. A cute joey fits comfortably and cosily in the front pouch.

Kangaroo Bag

FINISHED SIZE

Approximately 38 cm (15 in) long × 36 cm (14¼ in) at widest point

MATERIALS

- **Jaeger** *Natural Fleece*
  Two balls of Cameo 521 (MC)
- **Rowan** *Big Wool*
  Two balls of Cream 01 for tummy (A)
- **Debbie Bliss** *Cashmerino Aran*
  Two balls of Brown 300105 for nose and eyes (B)
- Hook: 10.00 mm (N-15) and 5.00 mm (H-8)
- Yarn needle

TENSION

5 sts and 5 rows measured over 5 cm (2 in) working in double crochet in yarn MC and using 10.00 mm (N-15) hook.

NOTE:

Before beg the second rnd in each section, place a marker or short length of contrasting yarn across your crochet and up against the loop on the hook and above the working yarn. Work Rnd 2, then slip the marker out and place it at the beg of the next rnd and so on. The marker will indicate where each subsequent rnd starts.

BAG

Foundation row: Using yarn MC and 10.00 mm (N-15) hook, beg at the round base, make 2ch.

Rnd 1: 6dc in 2nd ch from hook.

Rnd 2: 2dc in each of next 6dc (12 dc).

Rnd 3: *1dc in next dc, 2dc in next dc, rep from * around (18 dc).

Rnd 4: *1dc in each of next 2dc, 2dc in next dc, rep from * around (24 dc).

Rnd 5: *1dc in each of next 3dc, 2dc in next dc, rep from * around (30 dc).

Rnd 6: *1dc in each of next 4dc, 2dc in next dc, rep from * around (36 dc).

Rnd 7: *1dc in each of next 5dc, 2dc in next dc, rep from * around (42 dc).

Cont working in this patt for 5 rnds more, inc 1dc in each rep before the 2dc, until you have worked one rnd with 10dc, then 2 in each rep (72 dc).

Shape sides

Rnd 13: 1dc in each of next 72dc. Rep last round 4 times more.

Shape back

Row 1: 1ch, 1dc in each of next 40dc, turn.
Rep last row 7 times more.

Row 9: 1ch, *1dc in each of next 7dc, miss next dc, rep from * to end, turn (35 dc).

Row 10: 1ch, 1dc in each of next 35dc, turn.
Rep last row 7 times more.

Row 18: 1ch, *1dc in each of next 6dc, miss next dc, rep from * to end, turn (30 dc).

Row 19: 1ch, 1dc in each of next 30dc, turn.
Rep last row 7 times more.

Shape head flap

Row 27: 1ch, 1dc in each of next 22dc, turn.

Row 28: 1ch, 1dc in each of next 14dc, turn.
Rep last row once more.

Row 30: Sl st next dc, 1ch, 1dc in each dc to last 2 dc, miss next dc, 1dc in last dc, turn (12 dc).

Row 31: 1ch, 1dc in each dc across.

Rep last 2 rows 3 times more (6 dc).

Row 38: 1ch, 1dc in each of next 6dc, turn.

Rep last row twice more.

Make nose

Fasten off yarn MC, join in yarn B.

Rep last row 3 times more. Fasten off.

Shape front

With RS facing, join on yarn A with sl st in first dc of rem 32 dc left around last rnd of base.

Row 1: 1ch, 1dc in each of next 32 dc, turn.

Rep last row 7 times more.

Row 9: 1ch, *1dc in each of next 7dc, miss next dc, rep from * to end, turn (28 sts).

Row 10: 1ch, 1dc in each of next 28dc, turn.

Rep last row 7 times more.

Row 18: 1ch, *1dc in each of next 6dc, miss next dc, rep from * to end, turn (24 sts).

Row 19: 1ch, 1dc in each of next 24dc, turn.

Rep last row 7 times more.

Fasten off.

DRAWSTRING

Using yarn A and 10.00 mm (N-15) hook, make 100ch, fasten off. Weave in ends. Use this drawstring to weave in and out in every other dc along the top edge, both ends emerging at the centre front of bag.

POUCH

Foundation row: At the front of the bag at the point where yarn A joins yarn MC, on the next dc row join in yarn A and using 10.00 mm (N-15) hook, work 1dc in each of 12dc at centre of the front of the bag, turn.

Row 1: 1ch, 1dc in each of next 12dc, turn.

Rep last row 8 times more.

Fasten off, leaving a long tail end for sewing up the sides onto the front of the bag.

EARS

Make 2 alike.

Foundation row: Beg at the bottom of the ear – the end that is sewn onto the head. Using yarn A and 10.00 mm (N-15) hook and leaving a long tail end to sew onto the outer ear, make 10ch.

Row 1: 1tr in 4th ch from hook, 1tr in each of next 4ch, 1htr in next ch, [1dc, 1ch, 1dc] in last ch, cont along lower edge of ch, 1htr between htr and next tr, [1tr between next 2tr] 4 times, 1tr between last tr and 3ch at beg of row.

NOTE: *Do not fasten off.*

Border

Next rnd: 1ch, work in dc evenly around outer edge of ear, sl st to first dc. Fasten off.

STRAPS

Make 2 alike.

Foundation row: Using yarn A and 10.00 mm (N-15) hook, make 34ch.

Row 1: 1dc in 2nd ch from hook, 1dc in each ch to end, turn (33 dc).

Row 2: 1ch, 1dc in each dc to end, turn.

Rep last row once more. Fasten off leaving a long tail end for sewing on the straps.

TO FINISH

With RS facing and using yarn B and satin stitch, sew an eye to each side of the top of the head flap. Sew on the straps at the back of the bag, placing the tops of the straps 2dc apart at the centre of the back of the back just under the drawstring, then sew the other ends of the straps at the base of the bag where 'shape sides' begins and where yarn MC joins yarn A. Sew the base of the ears at the top of the head flap – 7dc apart, then sew the tip of the ears onto the strap, so that when the bag straps are held up the ears are held up, too.

Joey

FINISHED SIZE

Approximately 13 cm (5 in) tall

MATERIALS

- **Rooster** *Almerino DK*
  One ball of Hazelnut 202 (MC)
  One ball of Cornish 201 (A)
- **Debbie Bliss** *Cashmerino Aran*
  Small amount of Baby Pink 603
  for inner ear (B)

- Hook: 5.00 mm (H-8)
- Brown yarn or embroidery thread for eyes and nose
- Polyester toy fibrefill or wadding
- Yarn needle

TENSION

8 sts and 7 rows measured over 5 cm (2 in) working in double crochet in yarn MC and using 5.00 mm (H-8) hook.

HEAD

Foundation row: Beg at the nose, using yarn MC and 5.00 mm (H-8) hook, make 2ch.

Rnd 1: 6dc in 2nd ch from hook.

Rnd 2: 1dc in each dc around.

Rep last round twice more.

Rnd 5: *1dc in next dc, 2dc in next dc, rep from * around (9 dc).

Rnd 6: 1dc in each dc around.

Rnd 7: *1dc in each of next 2dc, 2dc in next dc, rep from * around (12 dc).

Rnd 8: 1dc in each dc around.

Rep last round twice more.

Rnd 11: *1dc in each of next 2dc, miss next dc, rep from * around (8 dc).

Stuff the head. Weave in end at the nose.

Rnd 12: *1dc in each of next 2dc, miss next dc, rep from * until the round is closed.

Fasten off and weave in end.

INNER EARS

Make 2 alike.

Foundation row: Beg at the bottom of the ear – the end that is sewn nearest to the head. Using yarn B, and leaving a long tail end for sewing onto the outer ear, make 10ch.

Row 1: 1tr in 4th ch from hook, 1tr in each of next 4ch, 1htr in next ch, [1dc, 1ch, 1dc] in last ch, cont along lower edge of ch, 1htr between htr and next tr, [1tr between next 2tr] 4 times, 1tr between last tr and 3ch at beg of row.

Fasten off, weave in end.

OUTER EARS

Make 2 alike.

Foundation row: Beg at the bottom of the ear – the end that is sewn nearest to the head. Using yarn MC, and leaving a long tail end for sewing onto the head, make 10ch.

Work as for inner ear from ** to **.

NOTE: *Do not fasten off.*

Border

Next rnd: 1ch, work in dc evenly around outer edge of ear, sl st to first dc. Fasten off, weave in end.

BODY

Foundation row: Beg at the bottom, using yarn MC, make 2ch.

Rnd 1: 6dc in 2nd ch from hook.

Rnd 2: 2dc in each of next 6dc (12 dc).

Rnd 3: 2dc in each of next 12dc (24 dc).

Rnd 4: 1dc in each dc around.

Rep last round 5 times more.

Shape back

Row 1: 1ch, 1dc in each of next 16dc, place marker, turn (16 dc).

Rep last row once more.

Row 3: 1ch, *miss next dc, 1dc in each of next 3 dc, rep from * across, turn (12 dc).

Row 4: 1ch, 1dc in each dc across, turn (12 dc).

Row 5: 1ch, *miss next dc, 1dc in each of next 2dc, rep from * across, turn (8 dc).

Row 6: 1ch, 1dc in each dc across, turn (8 dc).

Rep last row once more, fasten off.

Shape front

Row 1: Join in yarn A to dc at first marker, 1ch, 1dc in each of rem 8 dc at front, 1dc in next dc, turn (9 dc).

Row 2: 1ch, 1dc in each dc across, turn.

Row 3: 1ch, *miss next dc, 1dc in each of next 2dc, rep from * across, turn (6 dc).

Row 4: 1ch, 1dc in each dc across, turn (12 dc).

Row 5: 1ch, *miss next dc, 1dc in next dc, rep from * across, turn (3 dc).

Row 6: 1ch, 1dc in each dc across, turn (3 dc).

Rep last row once more, fasten off.

Sew up the row ends to join front to back, leaving the neck edges open.

Turn RS out.

Shape top

Rnd 1: Join in yarn MC with sl st in any dc at neck edge, 1ch, 1dc in each dc around (11 dc).

Rnd 2: 1dc in each of next 11dc.

Rep last rnd once more.

Rnd 4: 1dc in next dc, [miss next dc, 1dc in next dc] 5 times (6 dc).

Stuff the body.

Rnd 5: *1dc in each of next 2dc, miss next dc, rep from * until rnd is closed.

Fasten off leaving a long tail end – use this to sew the body to the head.

HIND LEGS

Make 2 alike.

Foundation row: Beg at toe, using yarn MC, make 2ch.

Rnd 1: 6dc in 2nd ch from hook.

Rnd 2: *1dc in next dc, 2dc in next dc, rep from * around (9 dc).

Rnd 3: 1dc in each dc around.

Rep last round 8 times more.

Shape heel

Row 1: 1dc in each of next 4dc, turn.

Row 2: 1ch, 1dc in each of next 4dc, turn.

Rep last round once more.

Fasten off. Join heel seam – fold the finishing row (last 4dc) in half so that the 2 ends meet and sew together to form back of heel.

Shape leg

Rnd 1: Join in yarn MC with a sl st at top of heel seam, 4dc along first row-end edge of heel, 1dc in each of 5dc across front of foot, then 4dc along 2nd row-end edge of heel (13 dc).

Stuff foot lightly.

Rnd 2: 1dc in each of next 13dc.

Rep last round 5 times more.

Rnd 8: *1dc in next dc, miss next dc, rep from * until the round is closed.

Fasten off, leaving a long loose end for sewing onto body.

ARMS

Make 2 alike.

Foundation row: Using yarn MC make 6ch.

Row 1: 1dc in 2nd ch from hook, 1dc in each of next 4ch, make 4ch (9 sts).

Fasten off. Weave in ends, leaving a tail end for sewing to the body.

TAIL

Foundation row: Beg at body end, using yarn MC, make 2ch.

Rnd 1: 6dc in 2nd ch from hook.

Rnd 2: *1dc in next dc, 2dc in next dc, rep from * around (9 dc).

Rnd 3: 1dc in each dc around.

Rep last rnd 9 times more.

Rnd 13: *1dc in each of next 2dc, miss next dc, rep from * around (6 dc).

Rep last rnd 4 times more.

Rnd 18: *1dc in next dc, miss next dc, rep from * until the rnd is closed.

Fasten off. Weave in end.

TO FINISH

Using matching yarn, sew each inner ear to the outer ears, matching top to top and bottom to bottom. Sew each ear to the back of the head.

With the toe end facing towards the front, sew one side of each leg to the body – refer to the photograph for actual placing.

Sew each arm to the front of the body at the top of the front shaping.

Sew the tail to the back of the body.

Using brown yarn or embroidery thread, stitch a French knot for an eye on each side of the head. Sew a row of straight satin stitches close together for the nose.

Jenna the Giraffe

With her snazzy, striped dress and fanciful scarf, Jenna's a gentle giant with a sweet tooth. This fun and whimsical giraffe boasts plenty of attitude and bold style. Subtle details – including her flirty embroidered eyelashes, spots along her neck, and a gingham bow around her horn – lend a bounty of personality and character.

Giraffe

FINISHED SIZE
49 cm (19¼ in) tall × 55 cm (21¾ in) wide with forelegs outstretched

MATERIALS
- **Jaeger *Roma***
  One ball of Orange 008 (MC)
  One ball of Brown 012 (A)
- **Artesano *Alpaca***
  Small amount of Inca Cloud 002 for hooves and mane (B)
- Hook: 5.00 mm (H-8) and 4.00 mm (G-6)
- Pink and brown embroidery thread or fine yarn for mouth and nose
- Two 6 mm (¼ in) black glass beads or similar for eyes
- Black thread for eyelashes
- 30 cm (12 in) × 6 mm (¼ in) ribbon
- Polyester toy fibrefill or wadding
- Yarn needle

TENSION
9 sts and 8 rnds measured over 5 cm (2 in), working double crochet in MC and using 5.00 mm (H-8) hook.

NOTE:
Before beg the second rnd in each section, place a marker or short length of contrasting yarn across your crochet and up against the loop on the hook and above the working yarn. Work Rnd 2, then slip the marker out and place it at the beg of the next rnd and so on. The marker will indicate where each subsequent rnd starts.

HEAD AND BODY
Foundation row: Beg at the nose, using yarn MC and 5.00 mm (H-8) hook, make 2ch.

Rnd 1: 6dc in 2nd ch from hook.

Rnd 2: [1dc in next dc, 2dc in next dc] 3 times (9 dc).

Rnd 3: 1dc in each of next 9dc.
Rep last rnd twice more.

Shape head

Rnd 6: [1dc in each of next 2dc, 2dc in next dc] 3 times (12 dc).

Rnd 7: 2dc in each of next 12dc (24 dc).

Rnd 8: 1dc in each of next 24dc.
Rep last rnd twice more.

Shape back of head

Rnd 11: *1dc in each of next 2dc, miss next dc, rep from * around (16 dc).

Rnd 12: *1dc in next dc, miss next dc, rep from * around (8 dc).

Shape top of neck

Row 1: 1ch, 1dc in each of next 4dc, turn.
Rep last row once more, ending with sl st in next dc.
Fasten off. Sew up finishing row at back of neck by folding last 4dc in half and sewing together.
Stuff the head, avoiding the tip of the nose. Flatten the tip of the nose with your finger and use the tail end on the foundation row to sew up the end with a few stitches. Weave in the end.

Shape neck

Rnd 1: Join on yarn MC with a sl st in a dc near seam, 1dc in each dc and row-end edge around neck, join into ring with sl st in first dc of rnd (9 dc).

Rnd 2: 1dc in each of next 9dc.
Rep last rnd 10 times more, stuffing the neck as you crochet.

Rnd 13: 1dc in each of next 4dc, 2dc in next dc, 1dc in each of next 4dc (10 dc).

Rnd 14: 1dc in each of next 10dc.
Rep last rnd twice more.

Rnd 17: 1dc in each of next 4dc, 2dc in

each of next 2dc, 1dc in each of next 4dc (12 dc).

Rnd 18: 1dc in each of next 12dc.

Rep last rnd twice more.

Rnd 21: 1dc in each of next 4dc, 2dc in each of next 4dc, 1dc in each of next 4dc (16 dc).

Shape body

Rnd 22: *1dc in next dc, 2dc in next dc, rep from * around (24 dc).

Rnd 23: *1dc in each of next 2dc, 2dc in next dc, rep from * around (32 dc).

Rnd 24: 1dc in each of next 32dc.

Rep last rnd 9 times more.

Shape bottom

Rnd 34: *1dc in each of next 7dc, miss next dc, rep from * around (28 dc).

Rnd 35: 1dc in each of next 28dc.

Rnd 36: *1dc in each of next 6dc, miss next dc, rep from * around (24 dc).

Rnd 37: 1dc in each of next 24dc.

Rnd 38: *1dc in each of next 5dc, miss next dc, rep from * around (20 dc).

Rnd 39: 1dc in each of next 20dc.

Rnd 40: *1dc in each of next 4dc, miss next dc, rep from * around (16 dc).

Rnd 41: *1dc in each of next 3dc, miss next dc, rep from * around (12 dc).

Stuff the body.

Rnd 42: *1dc in each of next 2dc, miss next dc, rep from * around (8 dc).

Rnd 43: *1dc in next dc, miss next dc, rep from * around until the ring is closed.

Fasten off and weave in the end.

EARS

Make 2 alike.

Foundation row: Beg at the base of the ear – where it joins the head, using yarn MC and 4.00 mm (G-6) hook, make 2ch.

Rnd 1: 6dc in 2nd ch from hook.

Rnd 2: [1dc in next dc, 2dc in next dc] 3 times (9 dc).

Rnd 3: 1dc in each of next 9dc, turn. Now work in rows.

Row 1: 1ch, 1dc in each of next 8dc, turn (8 dc).

Row 2: Sl st in first dc, 1ch, 1dc in each dc across, turn (7 dc).

Rep last row 6 times more.

Rim of ear

Next rnd: Work in dc evenly from the point around edge of ear and back to the point, sl st in first dc.

Fasten off.

HORNS

Make 2 alike.

Foundation row: Beg at the top of the horn, using yarn MC and 4.00 mm (G-6) hook, make 2ch.

Rnd 1: 3dc in 2nd chain from hook, sl st in first top of first dc, make 9ch.

Fasten off, leaving a tail end with which to sew on the head.

SMALL SPOTS

Make 2 alike.

Foundation row: Using yarn A and 4.00 mm (G-6) hook, make 4ch, join with sl st in first ch to form ring.

Rnd 1: Working over loose end, 1ch, 8dc into ring (8 dc).

Rnd 2: [1dc in next dc, 2dc in next dc] 4 times, sl st in top of first dc (12 dc).**

Fasten off. Pull up the centre tail end to close the ring, sew onto the neck with the other tail end.

BIG SPOTS

Make 2 alike.

Work as for 'Small Spots' up to ** (12 dc).

Rnd 3: [1dc in each of next 2dc, 2dc in next dc] 4 times, sl st in top of first dc (16 dc).

Fasten off. Pull up the centre tail end to close the ring, sew onto the neck and body with the other tail end.

HOOVES

Make 4 alike.

Foundation row: Using yarn B and 4.00 mm (G-6) hook, make 2ch.

Rnd 1: 8dc in 2nd ch from hook.

Rnd 2: 2dc in each of next 8dc (16 dc).

Rnd 3: 1dc in each of next 16dc.

Rep last rnd 5 times more.

Rnd 9: [1dc in next dc, miss next dc] 8 times, sl st in top of first dc (8 dc).

Fasten off.

HIND LEGS

Make 2 alike.

Foundation row: Using yarn A and 4.00 mm (G-6) hook, make 28ch.

**Row 1: 1dc in 2nd ch from hook, 1dc in each ch across, turn.

Rnd 2: 1ch, 1dc in each dc across, turn.

Rep last row twice more.

Fasten off. **

FORELEGS

Make 2 alike.

Foundation row: Using yarn MC and 5.00 mm (H-8) hook, make 28ch.

Make as for hind legs from ** to **.

TAIL

Foundation row: Using yarn MC and 4.00 mm (G-6) hook, make 10ch.

Fasten off.

Cut short lengths of yarn B and sew to one end of tail to create a fringe.

TO FINISH

Using yarn MC, stitch a French knot at either side of the head, then sew a bead under each knot to make the eyes. Using black sewing thread used double, sew a fan of short stitches above the French knot as eyelashes. Using brown embroidery thread or yarn, sew two straight stitches to the nose for nostrils. Using pink embroidery thread or yarn, sew a stem stitch mouth under the nose. Sew the ear base to the back/side of the head, sew the horns to the top of the head. Sew the chin to the neck, to pull head down slightly.

Sew up the back seam of each leg. Stuff each hoof, insert the legs just into open end of the hoof and sew in place – the legs may need pressing to stop them from curling, but check the yarn manufacturer's guidelines before doing so. Sew on the tail. Tie ribbon in a bow around one horn.

Gown & scarf

MATERIALS

- RYC *Cashcotton 4-ply*
  One ball of Cyclamen 00911 (MC)
- Rowan *Lurex Shimmer*
  One ball of Pewter 333 (A)
- GGH *Handknit Amelie*
  One ball of Magenta 004 for scarf (B)
- Hook size: 5.00 mm (H-8)
- Yarn needle

TENSION

13 sts and 12 rows measured over 5 cm (2 in), working double crochet in MC and using 5.00 mm (H-8) hook.

GOWN

(Back and front worked in one piece.)

Foundation row: Beg at the hem edge, using yarn MC, make 49ch.

Row 1: 1dc in 2nd ch from hook, 1dc in each ch across, turn (48 dc).

Row 2: 1ch, 1dc in each dc across, turn. Rep last row 3 times more.

Fasten off yarn MC, join in yarn A and rep last row 5 times more.

Fasten off yarn A, join in yarn MC and rep last row 5 times more.

Fasten off yarn MC, join in yarn A and rep last row 5 times more.

Fasten off yarn A, join in yarn MC and cont as follows:

Row 21: 1ch, *1dc in each of next 3dc, miss next dc, rep from * across, turn (36 dc).

Row 22: 1ch, 1dc in each dc across, turn (36 dc).

Rep last row twice more.

Row 25: 1ch, *1dc in each of next 2dc, miss next dc, rep from * across, turn (24 dc).

Row 26: 1ch, [1dc in each of next 4dc, miss next 6dc, make 6ch] twice, 1dc in each of next 4dc.

Fasten off.

TO FINISH

Using MC yarn, sew up the back seam, weave in ends.

SCARF

Foundation row: Using yarn B, make 35ch.

Row 1: 1dc in 2nd ch from hook, 1 dc in each ch across (34 dc).

Row 2: 1ch, 1dc in each dc across.

Fasten off. Weave in ends.

Mama Duck & Pompom Chick

Whether propped on a bookshelf or a bedside table, this maternal duck is a delightful addition to any child's room. The young hatchling is so easy to create out of pompoms, you may want to make him a couple more friends in your favourite colours!

FINISHED SIZES
Mama Duck: 30 cm × 15 cm (12 × 6 in)
Pompom Chick: 6 cm (2½ in) diameter

MATERIALS
- **RYC *Luxury Cotton DK***
  One ball of Tang 252 for Mama Duck (MC)
- **Adriafil *Angora Carezza***
  Small amount of Brown 87 for bill and legs (A)
  One ball of Orange 85 for feet and chick (B)
- Hook: 4.00 mm (G-6) and 3.50 mm (E-4)
- 4.5 cm (1¾ in) diameter pompom-maker, or two circular pieces of cardboard cut to 4.5 cm (1¾ in) diameter with 2 cm (¾ in) diameter hole cut out in the centre
- 3 cm (1¼ in) diameter pompom-maker, or two circular pieces of cardboard cut to 3 cm (1¼ in) diameter with 10 mm (³⁄₈ in) diameter hole cut out in the centre
- Polyester toy fibrefill or wadding
- Yarn needle

TENSION
9 sts and 10 rnds measured over 5 cm (2 in), working double crochet and using 4.00 mm (G-6) hook.

NOTE:
Before beg the second rnd in each section, place a marker or short length of contrasting yarn across your crochet and up against the loop on the hook and above the working yarn. Work Rnd 2, then slip the marker out and place it at the beg of the next rnd and so on. The marker will indicate where each subsequent rnd starts.

Mama Duck

HEAD & BODY
Using yarn MC and 4.00 mm (G-6) hook, beg at the top of the head, make 3ch.
Foundation rnd: Working over tail end, 8dc in 3rd ch from hook, join to top of 3ch with sl st to form ring (8 dc).
Shape beneath head
Rnd 1: 2dc in each of next 4dc, 1dc in each rem dc around (12 dc).
Rep last round once more (16 dc).

Rnd 3: 1dc in each of next 16dc.
Rep last rnd 3 times more.
Shape neck
Rnd 7: *1dc in each of next 3dc, miss next dc, rep from * around (12 dc).
Rnd 8: 1dc in each of next 12dc.
Rep last rnd twice more.
Shape body
Rnd 11: 1dc in each of next 4dc, 2dc in each of next 6dc, 1dc in each of next 2dc (18 dc).
Rnd 12: 1dc in each of next 18dc.
Rep last rnd twice more.
Rnd 15: [1dc in next dc, miss next dc] twice, [1dc in next dc, 2dc in next dc] 4 times, [1dc in next dc, miss next dc] twice, 1dc in each of next 2dc (19 dc).
Rnd 16: 1dc in each of next 19dc.
Rep last rnd twice more.
Rnd 19: 2dc in each of next 5dc, [1dc in each of next 2dc, 2dc in next dc] twice, [1dc in next dc, 2dc in next dc] 4 times (30 dc).
Rnd 20: 1dc in each of next 30dc.
Rnd 21: *1dc in each of next 2dc, 2dc in next dc, rep from * around (40 dc).
Rnd 22: 1dc in each of next 40dc.
Rnd 23: [1dc in next dc, miss next dc] 4

times, 2dc in next dc, [1dc in each of next 2dc, 2dc in next dc] 8 times, [miss next dc, 1dc in next dc] 3 times, miss last dc (41 dc).

Rnd 24: 1dc in each of next 41dc.
Rep last round 3 times more.

NOTE: *The next 6 rnds create the 'fan' tail.*

Rnd 28: [1dc in next dc, miss next dc] 4 times, [1dc in each of next 2dc, 2dc into next dc] 8 times, 1dc in each of next 2dc, [miss next dc, 1dc in next dc] 3 times, miss last dc (41 dc).

Rnd 29: 1dc in each of next 41dc.
Rep last two rnds twice more.

Rnd 34: 1dc in each of next 41dc.
Rep last rnd once more.
Fasten off.

WINGS

Make 2 alike.

Using yarn A and 4.00 mm (G-6) hook, beg at the top of the wing and starting with a long tail end, which will be used to tie up the wings at the back, make 15ch.

Row 1: 1dc in 2nd ch from hook, 1 dc in each ch across, turn (14 dc).

Row 2: 1ch, miss first dc, 1dc in each dc to last dc, miss last dc, turn (12 dc).
Rep last row 4 times more (4 dc).
Fasten off.

BILL

Using yarn A and 3.50 mm (E-4) hook, make 3ch.

Foundation rnd: Working over tail end, 8dc in 3rd ch from hook, join to top of 3ch with sl st to form ring (8 dc).

Rnd 1: 1dc in each dc around.

Rep last rnd 4 times more.

Fasten off.

LEGS

Make 2 alike.

Using yarn A and 4.00 mm (G-6) hook, make 23ch.

Row 1: 1dc in 2nd ch from hook, 1 dc in each ch to last ch, sl st in last ch.

Fasten off.

FEET

Make 2 alike.

Using yarn B and 4.00 mm (G-6) hook, make 12ch.

Row 1: 1 dc in 2nd ch from hook, 1 dc in each of next 4ch, make 6ch, 1 dc in 2nd ch from hook, 1 dc in each of next 4 ch, 1 dc in each of next 5ch, sl st in last ch.

Fasten off.

TO FINISH

Using a blunt-ended yarn needle and MC yarn, sew the tail end together, leaving a gap. Then stuff the head, neck, body and tail, manipulating the fibrefill to give the duck its shape. Sew the gap closed.

Stuff the bill lightly, then oversew the bill to the front of the head. Using yarn A, stitch a French knot eye to each side of the head.

Sew on each wing with one of the row ends joined to one side of the straight part of the back. The loose tail end can be tied to join the two points of each wing to hold in the chick.

Attach one of the ends of each leg to the underbelly, about 4 cm (1½ in) apart. Attach the other end to the middle of the 'T' shape of the foot.

Pompom Chick

Using the larger of the pompom templates and yarn B, wind the yarn around the two pompom templates from one end to the other. If using a cardboard template, place the two pieces together and wind the yarn through the hole in the centre until the yarn feels thick on the template. Cut in between the templates, attach a length of strong yarn between the open cut ends of the yarn, and tie firmly. Open and remove the templates. Trim the pompom as close as you can to the centre, creating a tail shape on one side.

Make the smaller pompom in the same manner, trimming it as short as you can. Using yarn A, sew on a closed eye at each side of the head. To make the bill, using yarn A and 3.50 mm (E-4) hook, make 4 ch, weave in the loose end, bend the bill in half, and sew the middle fold onto the front of the pompom.

Larry the Lobster

Bold and cheerful, this boisterous, double-crocheted lobster looks as comfortable on rocky, muddy shorelines as he does in your child's warm embrace. This snazzy scavenger may have giant claws and wiry legs, but he's deceptively cuddly!

FINISHED SIZE
41 cm (16 in) long × 38 cm (15 in) wide (claws outstretched)

MATERIALS
- **Lobster Pot** *Bulky*
  One ball of Lobster Bisque
- Two 6 mm (¼ in) black glass beads or similar for eyes
- Hook: 10.00 mm (N-15)
- Polyester toy fibrefill or wadding
- Yarn needle

TENSION
9 sts and 8 rnds measured over 5 cm (2 in), working double crochet in MC and using 10.00 mm (N-15) hook.

NOTE:
Before beg the second rnd in each section, place a marker or short length of contrasting yarn across your crochet and up against the loop on the hook and above the working yarn. Work Rnd 2 then slip the marker out and place it at the beg of the next rnd and so on. The marker will indicate where each subsequent rnd starts.

BODY
Foundation row: Beg at tail, make 9ch.
Row 1: 1dc in 3rd ch from hook, 1 dc in each of next 5ch, miss last ch, turn (6 dc).
Row 2 – 4: 1ch, 1dc in each dc across, turn.
Row 5: Make 6ch, miss first 5dc, sl st in last dc (12 sts).
Cont to work in rnds.
Rnd 1: 1dc in top of each of next 6dc, 1dc in each of next 6ch (12 dc).
Rnd 2: 1dc in each dc around.
Rep last rnd once more.
Rnd 4: 1dc in top of each dc around.
Rep last 3 rnds twice more.
Shape thorax
Rnd 11: *1dc in each of next 2dc, 2dc in next dc, rep from * around (16 dc).
Rnd 12: 1dc in each dc around.
Rep last rnd twice more.
Rnd 15: *1dc in each of next 3dc, miss next dc, rep from * around (12 dc).
Rnd 16: 1dc in each of next dc around.
Rep last rnd twice more.
Shape head
Rnd 19: *1dc in each of next 2dc, miss next dc, rep from * around (8 dc).

Rnd 20: [1dc in each of next 3dc, miss next dc] twice (6 dc).
Carefully turn out to other side, sew the edge of the abdomen at Rnd 1 to join with the top of the tail. Stuff the tail a little, then the body and the head.
Rnd 21: *1dc in next dc, miss next dc, rep from * until gap is closed.
Fasten off.

CLAWS
Make 2 alike.
Foundation row: Beg at the body end, make 2ch.
Rnd 1: 6dc in 2nd ch from hook.
Rnd 2 and 3: 1dc in each of next 6dc.
Rnd 4: *1dc in next dc, 2dc in next dc, rep from * around (9 dc).
Rnd 5: *1dc in each of next 2dc, 2dc in next dc, rep from * around (12 dc).
Rnd 6: *1dc in next dc, miss next dc, rep from * around (6 dc).
Shape large claw
Rnd 7: *1dc in next dc, 2dc in next dc, rep from * around (9 dc).
Rnd 8: 1dc in each of next 4dc, 2dc in next dc, 1dc in each of next 4dc (10 dc).

Rnd 9: 1dc in each of next 4dc, 2dc in each of next 2dc, 1dc in each of next 4dc (12 dc).

Rnd 10: 1dc in each of next 4dc, 2dc in each of next 4dc, 1dc in each of next 4dc (16 dc).

Rnd 11: 1dc in each of next 16dc.

Rnd 12: *1dc in each of next 3dc, miss next dc, rep from * around (12 dc).

Rnd 13: *1dc in each of next 2dc, miss next dc, rep from * around (8 dc).

Rnd 14: 1dc in each of next 8dc.

Shape large claw

Rnd 15: 1dc in each of next 8dc, turn. Cont to work in rows.

Row 1: 1ch, 1dc in each of next 5dc, turn. Rep last row once more.

Row 3: Sl st in first dc, 1ch, 1dc in

each of next 2dc, miss next dc, 1dc in last dc, turn (3 dc).

Row 4: Sl st in first dc, 1ch, 1dc in next dc (1 dc).

Fasten off.

SMALL CLAW

Foundation row: Beg at the body end, make 6ch.

Row 1: 1dc in 2nd ch from hook, 1dc in each ch across, turn (5 dc).

Row 2: Sl st in first dc, 1ch, 1dc in each of next 2dc, miss next dc, 1dc in last dc, turn (3 dc).

Row 3: Sl st in first dc, 1ch, miss next dc, 1dc in last dc, turn (1 dc).

Row 4: 1ch, 1dc in next dc.

Fasten off.

LEGS

Make 8 alike.

Foundation row: Beg at the body end, make 10ch.

Fasten off.

Snip one tail end to about 2 cm (¾ in), use the other to sew onto the body.

TO FINISH

For the rings around the tail, make three lengths of 16ch. Sew each chain of 16 around the tail along where rnds have been worked into top of dc only.

Cut two 30 cm (12 in) lengths of yarn for the antennae and sew to front of face, then sew the eyes just above these.

Sew up the large pincers along row ends, leaving a small gap for stuffing each claw. Stuff the first part of the claws, leaving pincers unstuffed. Close gaps, shape pincers to a point.

Sew the claws to the body near the eyes, referring to the photograph for positioning. Sew the legs, four on each side of the body, three pairs toward the head and last pair just above where the tail meets the body. Fold each small pincer in half widthways across the foundation row, sew up along row ends and lightly shape into a point with your fingers. Sew a small pincer to the top of each claw.

Sir Waldorf Walrus

Even though he's a softie, such a grand, formidable creature deserves a title of honour! Waldorf will quickly become a firm favourite amongst little ones. With his long tusks and soft belly, this creature of the deep makes an intriguing and fun playmate.

FINISHED SIZE
34 cm (13½ in) long

MATERIALS
- RYC *Cashsoft Aran*
  One ball of Mole 003 (MC)
  One ball of Cream 013 for cheeks (A)
- Anchor *Tapisserie Wool*
  One skein of 8036 (B)
- Hook: 6.50 mm (K-10½) and 5.00 mm (H-8)
- Two 5 mm (³⁄₁₆ in) buttons for eyes
- Brown yarn for nose
- Black sewing thread for whiskers and for attaching buttons
- Polyester toy fibrefill or wadding
- Yarn needle

TENSION
7 stitches and 6½ rows measured over 5 cm (2 in), working in double crochet in yarn MC and using 6.50 mm (K-10½) hook.

NOTE:
Before beg the second rnd in each section, place a marker or short length of contrasting yarn across your crochet and up against the loop on the hook and above the working yarn. Work Rnd 2, then slip the marker out and place it at the beg of the next rnd and so on. The marker will indicate where each subsequent rnd starts.

HEAD & BODY
Foundation row: Beg at the head, using yarn MC and 6.50 mm (K-10½) hook, make 2ch.
Rnd 1: 6dc in 2nd ch from hook.
Rnd 2: 2dc in each of next 6dc (12 dc).
Rnd 3: *1dc in next dc, 2dc in next dc, rep from * around (18 dc).
Rnd 4: *1dc in each of next 2dc, 2dc in next dc, rep from * around (24 dc).

Rnd 5: 1dc in each dc around.
Rep last rnd 5 times more.

Shape body

Rnd 11: 2dc in each of next 12dc, [1dc in next dc, miss next dc] 6 times (30 dc).

Rnd 12: 1dc in each dc around.
Rep last rnd 5 times more.

Rnd 18: 2dc in each of next 18dc, [1dc in next dc, miss next dc] 6 times (42 dc).

Rnd 19: 1dc in each dc around.
Rep last rnd 5 times more.

Rnd 25: *1dc in each of next 2dc, miss next dc, rep from * around (28 dc).

Rnd 26: 1dc in each dc around.

Rnd 27: *1dc in each of next 6dc, miss next dc, rep from * around (24 dc).

Rnd 28: 1dc in each dc around.

Rnd 29: *1dc in each of next 5dc, miss next dc, rep from * around (20 dc).
Stuff the walrus up to this row, then cont as follows:

Rnd 30: 1dc in each dc around.

Rnd 31: *1dc in each of next 4dc, miss next dc, rep from * around (16 dc).

Rnd 32: 1dc in each dc around.

Rnd 33: *1dc in each of next 3dc, miss next dc, rep from * around (12 dc).

Rnd 34: 1dc in each dc around.

Rnd 35: *1dc in each of next 4dc, miss next dc, rep from * around (6 dc).

Rnd 36: 1dc in each dc around.

Rep last rnd 5 times more.

Stuff the last of the body.

Rnd 42: *1dc in next dc, miss next dc, rep from * around until the ring is closed.

Fasten off.

CHEEKS

Make 2 alike.

Foundation row: Beg at the head, using yarn A and 5.00 mm (H-8) hook, make 2ch.

Rnd 1: 6dc in 2nd ch from hook.

Rnd 2: 2dc in each of next 6dc (12 dc).

Rnd 3: 1dc in each dc around.

Rnd 4: *1dc in next dc, 2dc in next dc, rep from * around (18 dc).

Rnd 5: 1dc in each dc around.

Rnd 6: *1dc in next dc, miss next dc, rep from * around (9 dc).

Stuff with a matching yarn to pad out.

Rnd 7: *1dc in next dc, miss next dc, rep from * until the ring is closed.

Fasten off.

FRONT FINS

Make 2 alike.

Foundation row: Using yarn A and 5.00 mm (H-8) hook, beg at the part of fin that is later sewn to body, make 8ch.

Row 1: 1dc in 2nd ch from hook, 1dc in each ch across, turn (7 dc).

Row 2: 1ch, 1dc in each dc across, turn.

Row 3: 2ch, 1tr in each dc across, turn.

Row 4: 2ch, 1htr in each of next 4tr, 1dc in each of next 3tr, turn.

Row 5: 1ch, 1dc in each of next 3dc, 1htr in each of next 4htr, turn.

Row 6: 2ch, 1htr in each of next 4htr, 1 dc in each of next 3dc.

Fasten off.

TAIL FINS

Make 2 alike.

Foundation row: Using yarn MC and 5.00 mm (H-8) hook, beg at the part of fin that is later sewn to body, make 5ch.

Row 1: 1dc in 2nd ch from hook, 1dc in each ch across, turn (4 dc).

Row 2: 1ch, 1dc in each dc across, turn.

Row 3: 2ch, 1tr in next dc, 1htr in next dc, 1dc in each of next 2dc.

Fasten off.

TUSKS

Make 2 alike.

Foundation row: Using yarn B and 5.00 mm (H-8) hook, beg at the part of fin that is later sewn to body, make 13ch.

Row 1: 1dc in 2nd ch from hook, 1dc in each ch across.

Fasten off, leaving the tail ends.

TO FINISH

Using matching yarn, sew the front fins onto each side of the body, curving the fin slightly as you stitch – so that you've sewn in an arc shape. Sew the two tail fins at either side at the end of the tail. Sew the cheeks onto the front of the head, then sew these together where they meet. Using brown yarn, oversew nose, catching the cheeks on each side. Using black thread, sew a few loose running stitches on each cheek to form whiskers.

Sew on the two button eyes at either side of the head. Sew on the tusks under the cheeks, using the tail ends – you may wish to press these with a cool iron if they curl a little, but check the yarn manufacturer's guidelines first.

Pinch the middle of the back to 'pull up' the walrus's back a little, then using matching yarn, sew a few discreet stitches to hold in place.

Mickey the Marmoset

Mickey's a cheeky character who will inspire your tot to have lots of fun. Soft, cuddly, and totally friendly with long, wraparound arms and legs and an endearing face – why not make a few more and create a playful troop of your own?

Marmoset

FINISHED SIZE

43 cm (17 in) long × 50 cm (19¾ in) wide (arms outstretched)

MATERIALS

- **Rowan** *Soft Baby*
  One ball of Princess 003 (MC)
- **Anchor** *Tapisserie Wool*
  One skein of Cyclamen Pink 8452 for head and body (A)
  Two skeins of Rose Pink 8454 for nose and tail (B)
- Hook: 5.00 mm (H-8)
- Small pieces of felt for eyes
- Black thread for sewing on eyes, nose and mouth
- Two 6 mm (¼ in) black glass beads or similar for eyes
- Polyester toy fibrefill or wadding
- Yarn needle

TENSION

12 sts and 9 rnds measured over 5 cm (2 in), working double crochet in MC and using 5.00 mm (H-8) hook.

NOTE:

Before beg the second rnd in each section, place a marker or short length of contrasting yarn across your crochet and up against the loop on the hook and above the working yarn. Work Rnd 2, then slip the marker out and place it at the beg of the next rnd and so on. The marker will indicate where each subsequent rnd starts.

HEAD & BODY

Foundation rnd: Using yarn A, beg at the nose end, make 4ch, join with a sl st to form ring.

Rnd 1: Working over tail end, [1dc in next ch, 2dc in next ch] twice (6 dc).

Rnd 2: 1dc in each of next 6dc.

Rnd 3: 2dc in each of next 6dc (12 dc).

Rnd 4: 1dc in each of next 12dc.
Break off yarn A.

Top of nose shaping

Rnd 5: Join in yarn MC, 2dc in each of next 10dc, 1dc in each of next 2dc (22 dc).

Rnd 6: 1dc in each of next 7dc, 2dc in each of next 5dc, 1dc in each of next 10dc (27 dc).
Break off yarn MC.

Rnd 7: Join in yarn B, 1dc in each of next 27dc.
Rep last round 3 times more.

Rnd 11: *1dc in each of next 2dc, miss next dc, rep from * around (18 dc).
Rep last round once more (12 dc).

Rnd 13: 1dc in each of next 12dc.
Rep last round once more.
Break off yarn B.

Rnd 15: Join in yarn MC, 1dc in each of next 12dc.
Stuff the head.

Body shaping

Rnd 16: *1dc in next dc, 2dc in next dc, rep from * around (18 dc).

Rnd 17: 1dc in each dc around.

Rep last 2 rnds once more (27 dc).

Rnd 20: 1dc in each dc around.
Rep last rnd 9 times more.

Rnd 30: *1dc in each of next 2dc, miss next dc, rep from * around (18 dc).
Rep last rnd once more (12 dc).
Stuff the body.

Rnd 32: Sl st every other dc around until the body opening is closed. Fasten off.

EARS

Make 2 alike.

Foundation rnd: Using yarn MC, make 4ch, join with a sl st to form ring.

Rnd 1: Working over tail end, [1dc in next ch, 2dc in next ch] twice (6 dc).

Next row: 2dc in each of next 6dc, turn (12 dc).

Next row: [1dc in each of next 2dc, miss next dc] 4 times (8 dc).
Fasten off.

ARMS

Make 2 alike.
Using yarn MC make 3ch.

Foundation rnd: Working over tail end, 8dc in 3rd ch from hook (8 dc).

Rnd 1: 1dc in each of next 8dc.

Rnd 2: 2dc in each of next 8dc (16 dc).

Rnd 3: *1dc in next dc, miss next dc, rep from * around (8 dc).

Rnd 4: 1dc in each of next 8dc.
Stuff hands.

Rep last rnd until arm measures 16 cm (6½ in).

Next rnd: *1dc in next dc, 2dc in next dc, rep from * around (12 dc).

Rnd 2: 1dc in each of next 12dc.
Rep last rnd until the entire arm measures 24 cm (9½ in).
Fasten off.

LEGS

Make 2 alike.
Using yarn MC make 4ch.

Foundation rnd: Working over tail end, 12dc in 4th ch from hook (12 dc).

Rnd 1: 1dc in each of next 12dc.

Rnd 2: 2dc in each of next 12dc (24 dc).

Rnd 3: 1dc in each of next 24dc.
Rep last rnd twice more.

Rnd 6: *1dc in next dc, miss next dc, rep from * around (12 dc).

Rnd 7: 1dc in each of next 12dc.
Stuff foot.
Rep last rnd until the entire leg measures 24 cm (9½ in).
Fasten off.

TAIL

Using yarn A, make 3ch.

Foundation rnd: Working over tail end, 12dc in 3rd ch from hook (12 dc).

Rnd 1: 1dc in each of next 12dc.
Rep last rnd until tail measures 21 cm (8¼ in). Break off yarn A.

Join in yarn MC and cont with the spiral until the entire tail measures 25 cm (9¾ in).
Fasten off.

TO FINISH

Using a blunt-ended yarn needle and MC yarn, sew two legs to the underside of the body equidistant from one another, and the two arms at either side of the body, two rows beneath the neck colour change. Sew the tail between the legs. Roll the first 12 cm (4¾ in) of tail into a coil and sew in place. Sew the base of each ear in place, referring to the photograph for positioning.

Cut out circles of felt 1 cm (½ in) in diameter for the irises. Sew a bead to the centre of each iris. Referring to the photograph for placement, sew on the eyes, taking care to sew through only one layer on the marmoset's face. Using black thread and stem stitch, sew on the mouth along first rnd of crochet. Satin stitch a nose in place above the mouth.

Overalls

MATERIALS

- **GGH *Big Easy***
  One ball of Red 005 (MC)
- Hook: 4.00 mm (G-6)
- Yarn needle

TENSION

13 sts and 10 rnds measured over 5 cm (2 in) working double crochet in MC and using 4.00 mm (G-6) hook.

SHORTS

Make 2 alike.

Foundation rnd: Using yarn MC, beg at the leg end, make 21ch, join with a sl st to form ring.

Rnd 1: 1ch (does not count as a st), 1dc in each ch around (21 dc).

Rnd 2: 1dc in each of next 21dc.

Rep last rnd 9 times more.

Now work in rows.

Leg shaping

Row 1: 1ch (counts as first st), miss next dc, 1dc in each of next 18dc, turn (19 sts).

Row 2: 1ch, miss next dc, 1dc in each of next 17dc, turn (18 sts).

Row 3: 1ch, miss next dc, 1dc in each of next 16dc, turn (17 sts).

Row 4: 1ch, miss next dc, 1dc in each of next 15dc, turn (16 sts).

Row 5: 1ch, miss next dc, 1dc in each of next 14dc, turn (15 sts).

Row 6: 1ch (does not count as a st), 1dc in each of next 14dc, 1dc in 1ch at beg of previous row, turn (15 dc).

Row 7: 1ch (does not count as a st), 1dc in each of next 15dc, turn.

Rep last row once more.

Fasten off.

TO FINISH

With RS facing, work 1dc along both edges of centre front and centre back shaping to join both front and back seam.

BIB

With RS and front of trousers facing, count 4dc along last row of left trouser leg, join in yarn MC to this st, 1ch, 1dc in each of next 4dc to front seam, 1dc in each of next 4dc along top of right trouser leg, turn (8 dc).

Next row: 1ch (does not count as a st), 1dc in each of next 8dc, turn.

Rep last row 4 times more.

NOTE: *Do not fasten off.*

Make 17ch for right strap, or until the strap goes from front (top of the bib) over the shoulders and down the back to join the back of the shorts at the waist – you may need to slip the overalls onto the marmoset to accurately measure this.
Fasten off.

Rejoin yarn to other corner of bib, make ch to match other strap and cross the straps over at the back, sew the straps in place at the waist.

Cocoa Koala

G'day, mate! This playful button-nosed marsupial knows how to hang loose. Donning a pretty blue sheath dress accented with pink bows, she's come a long way from home. Your little one is sure to hang onto her forever!

FINISHED SIZE
20 cm (7¾ in) tall

MATERIALS
- **Rowan** *Summer Tweed Aran*
  One ball of Hurricane 520 (MC)
- **Jo Sharp Yarns** *Kid Mohair*
  Small amount of Tranquil 609 for ears (A)
- Hook: 5.00 mm (H-8) and 4.00 mm (G-6)
- Dark grey DK yarn for nose
- Hot pink lightweight yarn or embroidery thread for mouth
- Yellow embroidery thread for ear bow
- Two 6 mm (¼ in) black glass beads or similar for eyes
- Polyester toy fibrefill or wadding
- Yarn needle

TENSION
9 dc and 8 rnds measured over 5 cm (2 in), working double crochet in MC and using 5.00 mm (H-8) hook.

NOTE:

Before beg the second rnd in each section, place a marker or short length of contrasting yarn across your crochet and up against the loop on the hook and above the working yarn. Work Rnd 2 then slip the marker out and place it at the beg of the next rnd and so on. The marker will indicate where each subsequent rnd starts.

HEAD

Foundation row: Beg at nose, using yarn MC and 5.00 mm (H-8) hook, make 2ch.

Rnd 1: 6dc in 2nd ch from hook.

Rnd 2: *1dc in next dc, 2dc in next dc, rep from * around (9 dc).

Rnd 3: 1dc in each dc around.

Rep last rnd twice more.

Shape head

Rnd 6: *1dc in each of next 2dc, 2dc in next dc, rep from * around (12 dc).

Rnd 7: 1dc in each dc around.

Rnd 8: *1dc in each of next 3dc, 2dc in next dc, rep from * around (15 dc).

Rnd 9: 1dc in each dc around.

Using dark grey DK yarn, sew on the nose working a few satin stitches across 3dc of first 3 rnds. Sew on the eyes on each side above the nose. Using pink yarn or embroidery thread, sew a straight stitch for mouth beneath the nose. Stuff the head.

Shape back of head

Rnd 10: *1dc in each of next 2dc, miss next dc, rep from * around (10 dc).

Rnd 11: *1dc in next dc, miss next dc, rep from * around until ring is closed.

Fasten off. Weave long tail end through to the inside of the head to come out under the chin.

EARS

Make 2 alike.

Foundation row: Using yarn A and 4.00 mm (G-6) hook, make 2ch.

Rnd 1: 6dc in 2nd ch from hook.

Rnd 2: *1dc in next dc, 2dc in next dc, rep from * around (9 dc).

Rnd 3: 1dc in each dc around.

Fasten off. Sew this end to the side of the head.

BODY

Make 2 alike.

Foundation row: Using yarn MC and 5.00 mm (H-8) hook, make 2ch.

Rnd 1: 6dc in 2nd ch from hook.

Rnd 2: 2dc in each of next 6dc (12 dc).

Rnd 3: 1dc in each dc around.

Rep last two rnds once more (24 dc).

Rnd 6: 1dc in each dc around.

Rep last rnd twice more.

Fasten off, leaving long tail end for sewing up front body to back.

ARMS

Make 2 alike.

Foundation row (RS): Beg at the top of the arm, using yarn MC and 5.00 mm (H-8) hook, make 16ch.

Row 1 (WS): 1dc in 2nd ch from hook, 1dc in each ch to end, turn (15 dc).

Row 2 (RS): 1ch, 1dc in each dc to end, turn.

Rep last row 3 times more.

Shape hand

Row 6 (RS): 1ch, 1dc in each of next 3dc, sl st in next dc.

Fasten off, leaving a tail end long enough for sewing the arm seam.

Join other half of hand

With RS facing and working along foundation row edge, count in 4ch from hand end, pull though yarn MC to 4th ch, 1ch, 1dc in each of next 3ch (3 dc).

Fasten off.

LEGS

Make 2 alike.

Foundation row: Beg at toe, using yarn MC and 5.00 mm (H-8) hook, make 2ch.

Rnd 1: 6dc in 2nd ch from hook.

Rnd 2: *1dc in next dc, 2dc in next dc, rep from * around (9 dc).

Rnd 3: 1dc in each dc around.

Rep last rnd 4 times more.

Shape heel

Row 8: 1dc in each of next 4dc, turn.

Row 9: 1ch, 1dc in each of next 4dc, turn.
Rep last row once more.
Fasten off.
Join heel seam – fold the finishing row (last 4dc) in half so that the two ends meet and sew together to form back of heel.

Shape top of foot

Row 11: Join in yarn MC with a sl st at top of heel seam, 1ch, 1dc in heel seam, 3dc along first row-end edge of heel, dc in each of 5dc across front of foot, then 3dc along 2nd row-end edge of heel (12 dc).

Row 12: 1ch, 1dc in each of next 12dc, turn.
Rep last row until the leg measures 9 cm (3½ in) from toe.
Fasten off, leaving long tail end for sewing up back seam.

TO FINISH

Sew the two body pieces together, RS facing, leaving a gap for turning through. Turn RS out and stuff. Close the gap. Sew the underside of the head to the body.
With WS facing, sew up the arms along the seams, leaving a small gap at the hands. Stuff the hands lightly, close the gap. Join to the body just beneath where the head is attached. Lay one hand over the other and sew together at centre.

Turn each leg WS out, sew up seam. Turn out right way.
Sew a leg to each side of the body with toes pointing to front.
Using a short length of yellow embroidery thread, tie a bow at top of left ear.

Dress

MATERIALS

- **GGH** *Big Easy*
  One ball of Turquoise 021 for top (MC)
- **RYC** *Cashsoft Aran*
  Small amount of Midnight 008 (A)
- Small amounts of any DK yarn for the bows on dress
- Hook: 5.00 mm (H-8)
- Yarn needle

TENSION

9 dc and 8 rnds measured over 5 cm (2 in), working double crochet in MC using 5.00 mm (H-8) hook.

Foundation row: Beg at the neck edge, using yarn A, make 16ch.
Row 1: 1dc in 2nd ch from hook, 1 dc in each ch to end, join into a ring with sl st in first dc of rnd, taking care not to twist chain (15 dc).
Rnd 1 (Row 2): 1ch, 1dc in each dc around.

Make armholes

Rnd 2: 1dc in each of next 3dc, miss next 2dc, make 2ch, 1dc in each of next 5dc, miss next 2dc, make 2ch, 1dc in each of next 3dc, ending with sl st in top of first dc.
Fasten off yarn A.
Join in yarn MC to same place as sl st was worked.
Rnd 3: 1dc in each of next 3dc, 2dc in next 2ch sp, 1dc in each of next 5dc, 2dc in next 2ch sp, 1dc in each of next 3dc (15 dc).
Rnd 4: *1dc in each of next 2dc, 2dc in next dc, rep from * to end (20 dc).
Rnd 5: 2dc in each dc around (40 dc).
Rnd 6: 1dc in each dc around.
Rep last row 5 times more, ending sl st in first dc of rnd, finishing at the back of the dress.
Fasten off and weave in ends.
Tie five small bows over the dress to embellish.

Farmyard & Nursery Toys

Our farmyard friends are designed to be interactive and love to tell bedtime stories. A few nursery toys will add warmth to your child's bedroom and help send your tot to the land of sweet dreams.

Magical Finger Puppets

Easy to make, these four magical characters get a thumb's up on fun! Create the ones here or design your own characters from your favourite film or book. They really are a handful!

FINISHED SIZE
8 × 7 cm (3 × 2¾ in) tall

MATERIALS

Wizard
- **Adriafil *Angora Carezza***
  Small amount of Blue 22 (MC)
- **Jaeger *Baby Merino 4-ply***
  Small amount of Dream 123 (A)
- **Anchor *Tapisserie Wool***
  Small amount of 8002 for wizard's beard
- Black sewing thread for eyes
- Small amount of silver metallic yarn

Witch
- **Twilley's *Freedom Cotton DK***
  Small amount of Black 14 (MC)
- **Jaeger *Baby Merino 4-ply***
  Small amount of Dream 123 (A)
- **Opal *Uni 4-ply***
  Small amount of Grass Green for hair
- Black sewing thread for eyes and nose
- Orange sewing thread for mouth

Owl
- **RYC *Cashsoft DK (light worsted)***
  Small amount of Cream 00500 (MC)

- **Anchor *Tapisserie Wool***
  Small amount of Cream 8036 for outer eyes (A)
- Small pieces of yellow felt
- Two white feathers
- Black sewing thread for eyes and nose

Walrus Calf
- **Adriafil *Angora Carezza***
  Small amount of Mole 87 (MC)
- **Rowan *Kid Silk Haze***
  Small amount of Pearl 590 (A)
- Cream yarn for tiny tusks
- Embroidery thread for sewing eyes, nose and mouth
- Two 6 mm (¼ in) black glass beads or similar for eyes

All versions
Hook: 4.00 mm (G-6)

TENSION
12 sts and 12 rows measured over 5 cm (2 in), working double crochet in MC and using 4.00 mm (G-6) hook.

NOTE:
Before beg the second rnd in each section, place a marker or short length of contrasting yarn across your crochet and up against the loop on the hook and above the working yarn. Work Rnd 2, then slip the marker out and place it at the beg of the next rnd and so on. The marker will indicate where each subsequent rnd starts.

Wizard, Witch & Owl

HEAD & BODY
Foundation row: Using yarn MC, make 12ch. Taking care not to twist the chain, join into a ring with sl st in first ch of rnd.
Rnd 1: 1ch, 1dc in each ch around (12 dc).
Rnd 2: 1dc in each dc around.
Rep last row until the body measures 5 cm (2 in).
Shape neck
Next rnd: *Miss next dc, 1dc in each of next 2dc, rep from * around (8 dc).
Next rnd: 1dc in each dc around.
Rep last rnd once more.
Witch and wizard only
Fasten off yarn MC with sl st in next dc, join in yarn A with sl st in same place, make 1ch.
Witch, wizard and owl
Next rnd: 1dc in each dc around (8 dc).

Next rnd: *2dc in next dc, 1dc in each of next 3dc, rep from * once more (10 dc).
Next rnd: *2dc in next dc, 1dc in each of next 4dc, rep from * once more (12 dc).
Next rnd: *2dc in next dc, 1dc in each of next 5dc, rep from * once more (14 dc).
Witch and wizard only
Use this to coil around in a flat twist at the end of the head. Sew in place to secure. Proceed to instructions for hat.
Owl only
*Miss next dc, 1dc in each of next 6dc, rep from * once more (12 dc).
Next rnd: *Miss next dc, 1dc in each of next 2dc, rep from * around (8 dc).
Next rnd: *Miss next dc, 1dc in next dc, rep from * around until the ring is closed. Fasten off. Weave in ends.

HAT – WITCH & WIZARD ONLY
Fasten off yarn A with sl st in next dc, join in yarn MC with sl st in same place, 1ch.
Next rnd: 1dc in each dc around.
Next rnd: *Miss next dc, 1dc in next dc, rep from * around (7 dc).
Next rnd: 1dc in each dc around.
Rep last rnd twice more.
Next rnd: *Miss next dc, 1dc in next dc,

rep from * around until the ring is closed. Fasten off. Weave in ends.

Witch's hat brim
Foundation row: Using yarn MC, make 15 ch.
Row 1: 1dc in 2nd ch from hook, 2dc in next ch, *1dc in next ch, 2dc in next ch; rep from * to end.
Fasten off. Sew the brim to the top of the head – where the hat rim colour begins.

WIZARD & WITCH'S CLOAKS
Foundation row: Beg at the top of collar, using yarn MC, make 11ch.
Row 1: 1dc in 2nd ch from hook, 1dc in each of next 7ch, miss last ch, turn (8 dc).

Row 2: Sl st in first dc, 1ch, 1dc in each of next 6dc, miss last dc, turn (6 dc).
Row 3: 1ch, 1dc in each dc across, turn. Rep last row 3 times more.
Row 7: 2ch, 1dc in 2nd ch from hook, 1dc in each dc to last dc, 2dc in last dc, turn (8 dc).
Rep last row twice more (12 dc).
Fasten off.
Work a border along each side edge starting at the hem corner and working up to the collar edge – 1dc in each dc along.
Fasten off. Weave in ends. Sew in place around the neck edge of the body, leaving upper collar edge free around the back of the head.

Using 2 short lengths of MC, make a tie at each side of collar and tie at front of cloak.

Using silver metallic yarn, sew a few stars working 3 straight stitches across each other onto the Wizard's robes, cloak and hat.

TO FINISH
Witch & Wizard
Using double thickness black sewing thread, sew two eyes on front of face. Work a split stitch mouth on Witch's face using a length of orange sewing thread. In cream yarn, work 2 straight stitches on Wizard's face for eyebrows.

For the Wizard's beard, cut 3 cm (1½ in) lengths of cream yarn. Thread half of one length through a stitch on the face at the beard position. Reinsert, then re-emerge the needle into the same crochet stitch – the thread should be secure. Trim if necessary. Work a few more lengths in the same way, depending on how bushy you want the beard to be.

For the Witch's hair, cut 3 cm (1½ in) lengths of hair yarn and attach to the back of the head – under the hat brim – in the same way.

Owl
Using outer eye yarn A, make 6ch, join into a ring with a sl st in first ch. Fasten off.

Make another the same and sew both in place onto the front of the head. Using black thread, sew two eyes into the centre of these outer eyes – making the eyes bigger than that of the wizard's and witch's. Cut out a 6 mm (¼ in) equilateral triangle of felt for the beak. Sew onto the owl's face with two black stitches for nostrils. Poke the ends of the feathers into the owl's neck at the side of the body. Sew in place.

Walrus calf

HEAD & BODY
Foundation row: Beg at the head, using yarns MC and A together, make 2 ch.
Rnd 1: 6dc in 2nd ch from hook.
Rnd 2: [1dc in next dc, 2dc in next dc] 3 times (9 dc).
Rnd 3: 1dc in each dc around.
Rep last rnd 3 times more.
Rnd 7: [1dc in next dc, 2dc in next dc] 4 times, 1 dc in last dc (13 dc).
Rnd 8: 1dc in each dc around.
Rep last rnd 3 times more.
Rnd 12: [1dc in each of next 3dc, 2dc in next dc] 3 times, 1 dc in last dc (16 dc).
Rnd 13: 1dc in each dc around.
Rep last rnd once more.
Rnd 15: *1dc in next dc, miss next dc, rep from * around (8 dc).
Rep last rnd twice more (2 dc).

Fasten off. Weave in loose ends.

CHEEKS
Make 2 alike.
Using yarn MC, make 7ch. Fasten off. Use this to coil around in a flat twist at the end of head. Sew in place to secure.

FLIPPERS
Make 2 alike.
Foundation row: In yarn MC, beg at the part of fin which is later sewn to body, make 5ch.
Row 1: 1dc in 2nd ch from hook, 1dc in each of next 3ch, turn (4 dc).
Row 2: 1ch, 1dc in each dc across, turn.
Row 3: 1ch, 1dc in each of next 3dc, turn (3 dc).
Row 4: 1ch, 1dc in each dc across, turn.
Row 5: 1ch, 1dc in each of next 2dc, turn (2 dc).
Row 6: 1ch, miss next dc, 1dc in last dc. Fasten off.

TO FINISH
Sew on the two beads for eyes behind the cheeks. Cut two short lengths of cream yarn and sew securely in place under the cheeks for tusks.
Sew on the flippers with the pointed end facing away from the head. Weave in ends.

Chunky Building Blocks

It's a block party! Learning your A-B-Cs from your 1-2-3s is made super-easy with these pastel blocks. It's a great way to use up a yarn stash and a fun accent for any nursery setting.

FINISHED SIZE

All blocks are different sizes as I used different types of yarn and hooks. This is a great way to use up any leftover yarn from other projects.

MATERIALS

- **Karabella** *Aurora Bulky*
  Small amount of Egg Cream 8 for yellow cube
- **Lobster Pot** *Bulky*
  Small amount of Hydrangea for turquoise cube
- **Rowan** *Soft Baby*
  Small amount of Angel 002 for pale blue cube
- Small amounts of any DK or tapestry yarn for letters and numbers
- Hook: 5.00 mm (H-8), 5.50 mm (I-9), 8.00 mm (L-12) and 10.00 mm (N-15)
- Polyester toy fibrefill or wadding
- Yarn needle

TENSION

Tension is not important for this project as any DK, Chunky or Super Chunky yarn can be used with appropriate hook sizes.

BLOCK

Foundation row: Using any yarn and a suitably sized hook, make 6ch.
Row 1: 1dc in 2nd ch from hook, 1dc in each ch across, turn (5 dc).
Rows 2–4: 1ch, 1dc in each dc across, turn (5 dc).
Rnd 5: 1ch, 1dc in each of next 4dc, 3dc in next (corner) dc, cont around edge making 3dc along left side, 3dc in corner, 3dc across bottom, 3dc in corner, 3dc along right side, 2dc in top right-hand corner, sl st to first dc of rnd.
Weave in ends. Make 5 more squares.

LETTERS & NUMBERS

Decide on a letter or number. Make enough chain to twist and curve into that shape, stitch the chain down onto one or more of the cube faces to secure the shape. For example:
For number '3', using

5.00 mm (H-8) hook, make 18ch, fasten off, leaving a long tail end to sew onto a cube face.

TO FINISH

Sew squares together along outside edges, WS together, and stuff before closing the cube along last edge.

Plush Car & Van

Make a chunky, bright blue bubble car and butter-yellow van, or try crocheting one in racy red, marmalade orange or bubblegum pink. Pick a colour to suit your mood – or your child's room!

Car

FINISHED SIZE

20 cm (7¾ in) long × 11 cm (4¼ in) wide

MATERIALS

- **Brown Sheep Company** *Lambs Pride Worsted*
  One ball of Brite Blue M-57 for car (MC)
  Small amount of Crème M-10 for roof (A)
- **Cottage Knits** *Chenille*
  One ball of Black for tyres (B)
- **Karabella Yarns** *Vintage Cotton*
  Small amount of Calendula 320 for headlights (C)
- Dark grey yarn for window and door detail
- Light grey yarn for door handle detail
- Hook: 5.00 mm (H-8) and 4.00 mm (G-6)
- Polyester toy fibrefill or wadding
- Yarn needle

TENSION

9 sts and 10 rnds measured over 5 cm (2 in), working double crochet in MC and using 5.00 mm (H-8) hook.

NOTE:

Before beg the second rnd in each section, place a marker or short length of contrasting yarn across your crochet and up against the loop on the hook and above the working yarn. Work Rnd 2, then slip the marker out and place it at the beg of the next rnd and so on. The marker will indicate where each subsequent rnd starts.

SIDES

Make 2 alike.
Foundation row: Beg at the back of the car, using yarn MC and 5.00 mm (H-8) hook, make 8ch.
Row 1: 1dc in 2nd ch from hook, 1dc in each ch across, turn (7 dc).
Row 2: 1ch, 1dc in each dc to last dc, 2dc in last dc, turn (8 dc).
Row 3: 2ch, 1dc in 2nd ch from hook, 1dc in each dc across (9 dc).
Rep last 2 rows once more (11 dc).
Row 6: 1ch, 1dc in each of next 11dc across, turn.
Row 7: 2ch, 1dc in 2nd ch from hook, 1dc in each dc across (12 dc).
Row 8: 1ch, 1dc in each of next 12dc across, turn.
Rep last row 8 times more.

Row 17: Sl st in first dc, 1ch, 1dc in each dc to end, turn (11 dc).
Row 18: 1ch, 1dc in each dc to last dc, miss last dc, turn (10 dc).
Rep last 2 rows twice more (6 dc).
Row 23: 1ch, 1dc in each of next 6dc, turn.
Row 24: 1ch, 1dc in each dc to last dc, miss last dc, turn (5 dc).
Row 25: 1ch, 1dc in each of next 5dc, turn.
Rep last row twice more.
Fasten off.

BASE

Foundation row: With yarn MC and 5.00 mm (H-8) hook, make 9ch.
Row 1: 1dc in 2nd ch from hook, 1dc in each ch across, turn (8 dc).
Row 2: 1ch, 1dc in each dc across, turn.
Rep last row 17 times more, or until the length of the base matches the length of one of the sides.

ROOF

Foundation row: With yarn MC and 5.00 mm (H-8) hook, make 9ch.
Row 1: 1dc in 2nd ch from hook, 1dc in each ch across, turn (8 dc).

Row 2: 1ch, 1dc in each dc across, turn.
Rep last row 7 times more, fasten off
yarn MC with sl st.
Join in yarn A with sl st in sl st of
previous row.
Row 10: 1ch, 1dc in each dc across, turn.
Rep last row 9 times more, fasten off
yarn A with sl st.
Join in yarn MC with sl st in sl st of
previous row.
Rep last row 7 times more, or until the
length of the roof fits up the back, over
the top, and down to the front along
one of the car sides.

TYRES
Make 5 alike.
Foundation row: Using yarn B and
5.00 mm (H-8) hook, make 4ch.
Rnd 1: 8dc in 4th ch from hook, working
over loose end – pull up tight when the
tyre is complete to close the ring.
Rnd 2: 2dc in each dc around (16 dc).
Rnd 3: 1dc in each dc around.
Rep last rnd twice more.
Rnd 6: [1dc in each of next 2dc, miss next
dc] 5 times, 1dc in last dc (11 dc).
Rnd 7: [1dc in next dc, miss next dc] 5
times, 1dc in last dc (6 dc).

Carefully turn out to RS.

Rnd 8: *Miss next dc, 1dc in next dc, rep from * to end.

Fasten off.

HEADLIGHTS

Make 2 alike.

Foundation row: Using yarn C and 5.00 mm (H-8) hook, make 2ch.

Rnd 1: 6dc in 2nd ch from hook.

Rnd 2: 2dc in each dc around (12 dc).

Rnd 3: 1dc in each dc around (12 dc).

Rep last rnd once more.

Rnd 5: *Miss next dc, 1dc in next dc, rep from * to end (6 dc).

Carefully turn out to RS.

Rep last rnd once more.

Fasten off.

TO FINISH

With RS facing, join each side to the car 'roof'.

Sew the two headlights onto front of car. Using yarn A, sew 2 straight stitches to each headlight for highlight.

With RS facing, sew the base to the rem outer edges of the front, back and sides, leaving a small gap for turning through. Turn RS out, stuff, and close the gap.

Sew on the wheels – two each side and one on the trunk, making sure the wheels on opposite sides are equidistant. Thread a yarn needle with a length of dark grey yarn. Work backstitch down

sides for door and windows and across front for windscreen details, as seen in the photograph. Using light grey yarn, sew a straight stitch to each 'door' for handle detail.

Van

FINISHED SIZE

24 cm (9½ in) long × 12 cm (4¾ in) wide

MATERIALS

- **Sirdar** *Super Chunky*
  One ball of Egg Yolk Yellow 906 (MC)
- **Karabella** *Aurora Bulky*
  One ball of White 3 (A)
  One ball of Grey 17 for wheels (B)
- **Debbie Bliss** *Cashmerino Chunky*
  Small amount of Grey 11 for headlights and bumpers (C)
  Grey yarn for window and door detail
- Hook: 6.50 mm (K-10½) and 4.00 mm (G-6)
- Polyester toy fibrefill or wadding
- Yarn needle

TENSION

7 sts and 6 rows measured over 5 cm (2 in), working double crochet in MC and using 6.50 mm (K-10½) hook.

BACK

Foundation row: Using yarn MC and 6.50 mm (K-10½) hook, make 11ch.

Row 1: 1dc in 2nd ch from hook, 1dc in each ch across, turn (10 dc).

Row 2: 1ch, 1dc in each dc to end, turn.

Rep last row 5 times more.

Change to yarn A, work 4 more rows as last row.

Fasten off.

LEFT SIDE, TOP & RIGHT SIDE

Foundation row: Beg at left back, using yarn MC and 6.50 mm (K-10½) hook, make 19ch.

Row 1: Sl st in first ch, 1ch, 1dc in each ch across, turn (18 dc).

Row 2: 1ch, 1dc in each dc across, turn.

Row 3: Sl st in first dc, 1ch, 1dc in each dc across, turn (17 dc).

Row 4: 1ch, 1dc in each dc across, turn.

Rep last row 3 times more.

Row 8: Change to yarn A, sl st in first dc, 1ch, 1dc in each dc across (16 dc).

Work 15 more rows as Row 4.

Row 24: Change to yarn MC, 1ch, 1dc in each dc to last dc, 2dc in last dc (17 dc).

Work 2 more rows as Row 4.

Row 27: 2ch, 1dc in 2nd ch from hook, 1dc in each dc across, turn (18 dc).

Row 28: 1ch, 1dc in each dc across, turn.

Rep last 2 rows once more (19 dc).

Fasten off.

FRONT

Foundation row: Using yarn MC and

6.50 mm (K-10½) hook, make 13ch.

Row 1: 1dc in 2nd ch from hook, 1dc in each ch across (12 dc).

Row 2: 1ch, 1dc in each dc to end, turn. Rep last row 7 times more.

Row 10: Sl st in first dc, 1ch, 1dc in each of next 9dc, miss next dc, 1dc in last dc (10 dc).

Row 11: Change to yarn A, 1ch, 1dc in each dc across.
Fasten off.

BASE

Foundation row: Using yarn MC and 6.50 mm (K-10½) hook, make 11ch.

Row 1: 1dc in 2nd ch from hook, 1dc in each next ch across, turn (10 dc).

Row 2: 1ch, 1dc in each dc across, turn. Rep last row 15 times more.
Fasten off.

Shape front dart

Foundation row: Using yarn A and 6.50 mm (K-10½) hook, make 12ch.

Row 1: 1dc in 2nd ch from hook, 1dc in each ch across, turn (11 dc).

Row 2: 1ch, 1dc in each dc across, turn. Rep last row twice more.

Row 5: Sl st in first dc, 1ch, 1dc in each of next 8dc, miss next dc, 1dc in last dc, turn (9 dc).

Row 6: Sl st in first dc, 1ch, 1dc in each of next 6dc, miss next dc, 1dc in last dc, turn (7 dc).

Row 7: Sl st in first dc, 1ch, 1dc in each of next 4dc, miss next dc, 1dc in last dc, turn (5 dc).

Row 8: Sl st in first dc, 1ch, 1dc in each of next 2dc, miss next dc, 1dc in last dc, turn (3 dc).

Row 9: Sl st in first dc, miss next dc, 1dc in last dc (1 dc).
Fasten off.

Join yarn MC to 1ch at corner of 'V'-shaped dart, work 1dc in row ends down two long sides to point of 'V'. Fasten off, leaving a long tail end for sewing the dart to the front of the van.

WHEELS

Make 5 alike.

Foundation row: Using yarn B and 6.50 mm (K-10½) hook, make 4ch.

Rnd 1: 10dc in 4th ch from hook.

Rnd 2: 2dc in each dc around (20 dc).

Rnd 3: 1dc in each dc around. Rep last rnd once more.

Rnd 5: [Miss next dc, 1dc in each of next 2dc] 6 times, miss next dc, 1dc in last dc (13 dc).

Rnd 6: [Miss next dc, 1dc in next dc] 6 times, miss last dc (6 dc).
Fasten off.

HEADLIGHTS

Make 2 alike.

Foundation row: Using yarn C and 4.00 mm (G-6) hook, make 4ch.

Rnd 1: 8tr in 4th ch from hook, sl st in top of first tr to form ring.
Fasten off, leaving long tail end for sewing to car.

BUMPERS

Make 2 alike.

Foundation row: Using yarn C and 4.00 mm (G-6) hook, make 21ch.

Row 1: 1dc in 2nd ch from hook, 1dc in each ch across, turn (20 dc).

Row 2: 1ch, 1dc in each dc across, turn. Rep last row 3 times more.
Fasten off. Roll up across the length as you would a sleeping bag, sew along one long end to secure.

TO FINISH

Using a blunt-ended yarn needle and MC yarn, backstitch throughout. Sew the dart to the front of the van. Sew on the two headlights. With RS facing, join the front to the van sides, join the back then the base leaving a small gap at the front for turning through. Stuff the van, then sew up the gap. Sew on the back and front bumpers and then the wheels, adding the fifth wheel to the bumper. Thread a yarn needle with a length of grey yarn. Work backstitch down sides for door and windows and across front for windscreen details. Using yarn A, embroider a French knot to each headlight for highlights. Using yarn C, embroider a door handle on each side.

Mama Horse & Foal

Mama Horse is a glove puppet, and her young foal is a delightful toy. They can cuddle together when it's time for a tea party or a bedtime story.

FINISHED SIZES

Mama Horse: 33 × 12 cm (13 × 4¾ in)
Foal: 26 × 26 cm (10¼ × 10¼ in)

Mama Horse

MATERIALS

- **Jaeger** *Baby Merino 4-ply*
  Two balls of Gold 225 (MC)
- **Artesano** *Alpaca*
  Small amount of Inca Cloud 002 (A)
- **Sirdar** *Snuggly DK*
  One ball of Lilac 219 for mane (B)
- Hook: 4.00 mm (G-6)
- Small pieces of felt in three colours for inner and outer eyes, and nose
- Thread for attaching felt and beads
- Two 6 mm (¼ in) black glass beads or similar for eyes
- Dark brown yarn for mouth
- Two dressmaker's pins
- Yarn needle

TENSION

9 sts and 10 rows measured over 5 cm (2 in), working double crochet in MC and using 4.00 mm (G-6) hook.

NOTE:

Before beg the second rnd in each section, place a marker or short length of contrasting yarn across your crochet and up against the loop on the hook and above the working yarn. Work Rnd 2, then slip the marker out and place it at the beg of the next rnd and so on. The marker will indicate where each subsequent rnd starts.

HEAD & BODY

Using yarn A, beg at the muzzle end, make 3ch.

Foundation rnd: Working over tail end, 8dc in 3rd ch from hook, join to top of 3ch with sl st to form ring (8 dc).

Rnd 1: 1dc in each of next 8dc.

Rnd 2: 2dc in each of next 8dc (16 dc).

Rnd 3: 1dc in each of next 16dc.

Rnd 4: *1dc in next dc, 2dc in next dc, rep from * around (24 dc).

Rnd 5: 1dc in each of next 24dc, sl st in top of first dc.

Shape muzzle

Rnd 6: 1ch, 1dc in same place as sl st was worked, 1dc in each of next 24dc (25 dc).

Rnd 7: Miss the sl st and the 1ch, work 1dc into top of first dc of previous rnd, 1dc into each of rem 24dc (25 dc).

Rnd 8: Change to yarn MC, 1tr in each of next 25dc, at the same time catching in the marker.

Rnd 9: 1tr in each of next 24tr, 2tr in last tr (26 tr).

Rnd 10: 1tr in each of next 26tr.

Rnd 11: 1tr in each of next 25tr, 2tr in last tr (27 tr).

Rnd 12: 1tr in each of next 27tr.

Rnd 13: 1tr in each of next 26tr, 2tr in last tr (28 tr).

Rnd 14: 1tr in each of next 28tr.

Rnd 15: 1tr in each of next 27tr, 2tr in last tr, sl st to top of first tr of rnd (29 tr).

Shape chin

Row 1: 2ch (counts as 1tr), miss tr where sl st was worked, miss next tr, 1tr in each of next 24tr, miss next tr, 1tr in next tr, turn (26 tr).

Row 2: 2ch (counts as 1tr), miss first 2tr, 1tr in each of next 23tr, 1tr in top of 2ch at beg of previous row, turn (25 tr).

Row 3: 2ch (counts as 1tr), miss first 2tr, 1tr in each of next 22tr, 1tr in top of 2ch at beg of previous row, turn (24 tr).

Row 4: 2ch (counts as 1tr), miss first 2tr, 1tr in each of next 21tr, 1tr in top of 2ch

at beg of previous row, turn (23 tr).

Row 5: 2ch (counts as 1tr), miss first tr, 1tr in each of next 20tr, 2tr in next tr, 1tr in top of 2ch at beg of previous row, join with sl st in top of 2ch at beg of row (24 tr).

Cont to work in spiral rnds (do not turn and keep with RS facing), placing marker at the beg of each rnd for 15 rnds at the same time increasing 2 sts on every third rnd as follows:

Rnd 3: 1tr in each of next 11tr, 2tr in next tr, 1tr in each of next 11tr, 2tr in last tr (26 tr).

Rnd 6: 1tr in each of next 12tr, 2tr in next tr, 1tr in each of next 12tr, 2tr in last tr (28 tr).

Rnd 9: 1tr in each of next 13tr, 2tr in next tr, 1tr in each of next 13tr, 2tr in last tr (30 tr).

Cont increasing as above until there are 34 tr.

Fasten off.

EARS

Make 2 alike.

Using 2 strands – yarn MC and A – together, make 3ch.

Foundation rnd: Working over tail end, 8dc in third ch from hook, join to top of 3ch with sl st to form ring.

Rnd 1: 1dc in each of next 8dc.

Rnd 2: 2dc in each of next 8dc (16 dc).

Rnd 3: 1dc in each of next 15dc, 2dc in next dc (17 dc).

Rnd 4: 1dc in each of next 17dc.

Drop yarn A and cont with yarn MC for the following rows:

Next row: 1dc in each of next 15dc, turn.

Next row: 1ch, miss first dc, 1dc in each of next 11dc, miss next dc, 1dc in next dc, turn (13 dc).

Rep last row 6 times more, working 2dc less before last dc on every row (1 dc).

Fasten off.

TO FINISH

With RS facing, using a blunt-ended yarn needle and matching yarn, backstitch the chin seam.

To mark where to sew on the ears, place the puppet over your hand (seam facing down), carefully pin two dressmaker's pins onto the crochet at the position where your wrist bends – the ears should lie 2.5 cm (1 in) apart with the inner ears facing outwards. Carefully take off the puppet and sew the ears in place, with matching yarn, around the first row of dc stitches.

Referring to the photograph as a guide, cut out two irises, two pupils and two nostrils from coloured felt.

Join each pupil to its iris by sewing a glass bead to the centre.

Referring to the photograph, sew on the felt nostrils and eyes with small stitches around the outer edges, taking care to sew through only one layer on the horse's nose. Using a short length of dark brown yarn, stem stitch a line across the nose to create the mouth.

To attach the mane, cut lengths of yarn B to about 10 cm (4 in). Taking two lengths at a time, bend both in half. Use a crochet hook to pull the loop through a tr stitch at the top of the head between the ears. Pass the cut ends through the loops, then pull the cut ends so that the knot lies at the top of the head. Continue with this fringing technique along the top of the head and a little way down the back of the neck.

Foal

MATERIALS

- **Rowan *Soft Baby***
  Two balls of Buttercup 008 (MC)
- **Sirdar *Snuggly DK***
  Small amount of Lilac 219 for mane and tail (A)
- **Adriafil *Angora Carezza***
  Small amount of Mink 87 (B)
- Hook: 5.00 mm (H-8) and 4.00 mm (G-6)
- Small pieces of felt in three colours for inner and outer eyes, and nostrils
- Thread for attaching felt and beads

- Two 6 mm (¼ in) black glass beads or similar for eyes
- Pink yarn for mouth
- Polyester toy fibrefill or wadding
- Yarn needle

HEAD & BODY

Using yarn A and 5.00 mm (H-8) hook, beg at the muzzle end, make 3ch.

Foundation rnd: Working over tail end, 8dc in third ch from hook, join to top of 3ch with sl st to form ring (8 dc).

Rnd 1: 1dc in each of next 8dc.

Rnd 2: 2dc in each of next 8dc (16 dc).

Rnd 3: 1dc in each of next 16dc.

Rep last rnd three times more, ending with sl st in top of first dc of rnd.

Rnd 7: Join in yarn MC to same place as sl st was worked, 1dc in each of next 16dc.

Shape nose

Rnd 8: 2dc in each of next 6dc, 1dc in each of next 10dc (22 dc).

Rnd 9: 1dc in each of next 22dc.

Rep last rnd 4 times more.

Rnd 14: [1dc in next dc, miss next dc] 6 times, 1dc in each of next 10dc (16 dc).

Rnd 15: 1dc in each dc around.

Shape chin

Rnd 16: [1dc in each of next 2dc, miss next dc] 5 times, 1dc in next dc (11 dc).

Rnd 17: 1dc in each dc around.

Rep last rnd once more.

Shape neck

Rnd 19: [1dc in each of next 3dc, 2dc in next dc] twice, 1dc in each of next 3dc (13 dc).

Rnd 20: 1dc in each dc around.

Rnd 21: [1dc in each of next 3dc, 2dc in next dc] 3 times, 1dc in next dc (16 dc).

Rnd 22: 1dc in each dc around.

Rnd 23: [1dc in each of next 3dc, 2dc in next dc] 4 times (20 dc).

Rnd 24: 1dc in each dc around.

Rep last rnd 3 times more.

Rnd 28: 1dc in each of next 5dc, [1dc in each of next 2dc, 2dc in next dc] 4 times, 1dc in each of next 3dc (24 dc).

Rnd 29: 1dc in each dc around.

Rep last rnd 3 times more.

Body shaping

Rnd 33: 1dc in each of next 8dc, 2dc in each of next 7dc, 1dc in each of next 9dc (31 dc).

Rnd 34: 1dc in each dc around.

Rnd 35: 1dc in each of next 10dc, 2dc in each of next 11dc, 1dc in each of next 10dc (42 dc).

Rnd 36: 1dc in each dc around.

Rep last rnd 4 times more.

Rnd 41: 1dc in each of next 11dc, [miss next dc, 1dc in next dc] 10 times, 1dc in each of next 11dc (32 dc).

Rnd 42: 1dc in each dc around.

Shape back

Rnd 43: [Miss next dc, 1dc in each of next 3dc] twice, 1dc in each of next 16dc, [miss next dc, 1dc in each of next 3dc] twice (28 dc).

Rnd 44: 1dc in each dc around.

Rnd 45: [Miss next dc, 1dc in each of next 3dc] twice, 1dc in each of next 12dc, [miss next dc, 1dc in each of next 3dc] twice (24 dc).

Rnd 46: 1dc in each dc around.

Rep last rnd 3 times more.

Shape hips

Rnd 50: [1dc in each of next 2dc, 2dc in next dc] 8 times (32 dc).

Rnd 51: [1dc in next dc, 2dc in next dc] 16 times (48 dc).

Rnd 52: 2dc in each of next 10dc, 1dc in each of next 28dc, 2dc in each of next 10dc (68 dc).

Rnd 53: 1dc in each dc around.

Rep last rnd 4 times more.

Rnd 58: *1dc in next dc, miss next dc, rep from * around (34 dc).

Rep last rnd once more (17 dc).

Stuff head and body.

Rnd 60: Sl st every other stitch around until opening is closed.

EARS

Make 2 alike.

Using yarn MC and 4.00 mm (G-6) hook, make 3ch.

Foundation rnd: Working over tail end, 8dc in third ch from hook, join to top of

3ch with sl st to form ring.

Rnd 1: 1dc in each of next 8dc.

Next row: 1dc in each of next 6dc, turn.

Next row: 1ch, 1dc in each of next 6dc, turn.

Next row: 1ch, miss first dc, 1dc in each of next 3dc, miss 1dc, 1dc in last dc, turn (4 dc).

Next row: 1ch, miss first dc, 1dc in next dc, miss next dc, 1dc in last dc, turn (2 dc).

Next row: Miss first dc, sl st in last dc. Fasten off. Turn ear inside out.

LEGS

Make 4 alike.

Beg with the hoof, using yarn B and 5.00 mm (H-8) hook, make 3ch.

Foundation rnd: Working over tail end, 8dc in third ch from hook, join to top of 3ch with sl st to form ring.

Rnd 1: 2dc in each of next 8dc (16 dc).

Rnd 2: 1dc in each of next 16dc. Rep last rnd twice more.

Shape front of hoof

Rnd 5: Miss first 2dc, 1dc in each of next 14dc (14 dc).

Rnd 6: Miss first 2dc, 1dc in each of next 12dc, sl st to first dc (12 dc). Break off yarn B.

Rnd 7: Join in yarn MC (leg colour) to same place as sl st was worked, 1dc in each of next 12dc, sl st to first dc.

Rnd 8: 1dc in each of next 12dc.

Shape hoof

Rnd 9: [1dc in next dc, miss next dc] 6 times (6 dc). Stuff hoof.

Rnd 10: 1dc in each of next 6dc. Rep last rnd 3 times more.

Shape knees

Rnd 14: [1dc in each of next 2dc, 2dc in next dc] twice (8 dc).

Rnd 15: [1dc in next dc, 2dc in next dc] 4 times (12 dc).

Rnd 16: 1dc in each of next 12dc.

Rnd 17: [1dc in each of next 2dc, miss next dc] 4 times (8 dc).

Rnd 18: [1dc in each of next 3dc, miss next dc] twice (6 dc).

Rnd 19: 1dc in each of next 6dc. Rep last rnd 5 times more.

Shape top of leg

Rnd 25: [1dc in next dc, 2dc in next dc] 3 times (9 dc).

Rnd 26: 1dc in each of next 9dc. Rep last rnd 3 times more.

Rnd 30: [1dc in each of next 2dc, miss next dc] 3 times (6 dc). Stuff lightly. Sl st every other stitch around until opening is closed.

TO FINISH

Using a blunt-ended yarn needle and MC yarn, sew the four legs to the underside of the body equidistant to one another.

Sew the base of each ear in place, referring to the photograph for positioning, taking care not to sew the two sides of the head together.

Referring to the photograph as a guide, cut out two irises, two pupils and two nostrils from coloured felt.

Join each pupil to its iris by sewing a glass bead to the centre.

Referring to the photograph, sew on the felt nostrils and eyes with small stitches around the outer edges, taking care to sew through only one layer on the horse's nose. Using a short length of pink yarn, stem stitch a line across the nose to create the mouth.

To attach the mane, cut lengths of yarn to about 10 cm (4 in). Taking two lengths at a time, bend both in half. Use a crochet hook to pull the loop through a dc stitch at the top of the head between the ears. Pass the cut ends through the loops, then pull the cut ends so that the knot lies at the top of the head.

Continue with this fringing technique along the top of the head and a little way down the back of the neck.

To attach the tail, follow the instructions for attaching the mane and make the strands twice as long.

Planets & Rocket Mobile

A charged, yarn rocket gently navigates colourful planets to take your little one to the outer limits of dreamland. It's the perfect project for using your yarn stash!

FINISHED SIZES

Planets: about 16 cm (6½ in) in diameter
Rocket: about 12 cm (4¾ in) long ×
    16 cm (6½ in) in diameter

MATERIALS

- **Karabella *Aurora Bulky***
  Small amounts of Hot Pink 5, Egg Cream 8, Pistachio 10, Shell Pink 9 for planets
- **Debbie Bliss *Cashmerino Aran***
  Small amount of Red 610 for planet
- **Rowan *Soft Baby***
  One ball of Angel 002
- **Sirdar *Chunky***
  Small amount of Yellow for planet
- **Frog Tree *Chunky***
  Small amount of Navy 37 for planet
- **Cottage Knits *Chenille***
  Small amount of Sky Blue for planet
- **GGH *Samoa-Mouline***
  Small amount of Violet 503 for rocket (MC)
- **Louisa Harding *Kashmir DK***
  Small amount of Lemon 5 for rocket (A)
- **RYC *Silk Wool DK***
  Small amount of Brownstone 308 for rocket base (B)

- Orange DK yarn for flames
- Pale blue DK yarn for hanging threads
- Hook: 6.50 mm (K-10½), 5.00 mm (H-8) and 4.00 mm (G-6)
- 20 cm (8 in) wooden hoop in diameter (or use one half of an embroidery hoop)
- 10 m (11 yd) of 10 mm (⅜ in) wide blue velvet ribbon
- Solvent-free glue stick for sticking the ribbon to the hoop
- Three 10 mm (⅜ in) diameter buttons
- Polyester toy fibrefill or wadding
- Yarn needle

TENSION

Tension is not important here.

NOTE:

Before beg the second rnd in each section, place a marker or short length of contrasting yarn across your crochet and up against the loop on the hook and above the working yarn. Work Rnd 2, then slip the marker out and place it at the beg of the next rnd and so on. The marker will indicate where each subsequent rnd starts.

PLANETS

Make 8 alike – 1 in each planet yarn.
Foundation row: Using any chosen planet yarn and 6.50 mm (K-10½) hook, make 4ch.
Rnd 1: 8dc in fourth ch from hook.
Rnd 2: 2dc in each dc around (16 dc).

Rnd 3: 1dc in each dc around.

Rep last rnd twice more.

Rnd 6: [1dc in each next of 2dc, miss next dc] 5 times, 1dc in last dc (11 dc).

Rnd 7: [1dc in next dc, miss next dc] 5 times, 1dc in last dc (6 dc).

Carefully turn out to RS and stuff the planet.

Rnd 8: *Miss next dc, 1dc in next dc, rep from * until ring is closed. Fasten off.

ROCKET

Foundation row: Using yarn MC and 5.00 mm (H-8) hook, make 2ch.

Rnd 1: 4dc in second ch from hook.

Rnd 2: 1dc in each of next 4dc.

Rnd 3: [1dc in next dc, 2dc in next dc] twice (6 dc).

Rnd 4: [1dc in next dc, 2dc in next dc] 3 times (9 dc).

Rnd 5: [1dc in next dc, 2dc in next dc] 4 times, 1 dc in next dc (13 dc).

Rnd 6: [1dc in next dc, 2dc in next dc] 5 times, 1dc in next dc (19 dc).

Rnd 7: 1dc in each dc around.

Rep last rnd twice more. Fasten off yarn MC with sl st in last dc.

Rnd 10: Join in yarn A with sl st in same place as last sl st. Using 4.00 mm (G-6) hook, 1dc in each dc around.

Rep last rnd 5 times more. Fasten off yarn A with sl st in last dc.

Rnd 16: Join in yarn B with sl st in same

place as last sl st. Using 5.00 mm (H-8) hook, 1dc in each dc around.

Rep last rnd 3 times more.

Fasten off.

ROCKET BASE

Foundation row: Using yarn B and 5.00 mm (H-8) hook, make 2ch.

Rnd 1: 4dc in second ch from hook.

Rnd 2: 2dc in each dc around (8 dc).

Rep last rnd twice more (32 dc).

Rnd 5: 1dc in each dc around.

Fasten off.

TO FINISH THE ROCKET

Stuff the rocket. Ease the base of the rocket to just inside the bottom of the rocket base – about 6 mm (¼ in) in. With MC yarn and yarn needle, sew in place. Sew the buttons in a line down the front.

Rocket boosters

Using yarn MC and 5.00 mm (H-8) hook, make 25ch, fasten off. Make another chain in the same manner. Wind one chain around your finger and sew to secure the coil. Do the same to the other chain. Sew each coil to the base of the rocket. Cut lengths of orange yarn and sew to the inside of each booster for flames. Trim.

TO FINISH THE MOBILE

Stick one end of the ribbon to the hoop to secure. Wrap the ribbon around the hoop until it is covered, then cut and secure the end with glue.

Cut the remaining ribbon into five equal lengths for hanging strips.

Glue one end of each of the five ribbon strips to the outside of the hoop at five evenly spaced points around the hoop. Knot the five lengths together at the other end.

Sew differing lengths of pale blue yarn to the top (finishing row) of each planet and to the rocket. Arranging the planets around the hoop as desired, knot each length of yarn securely to the hoop. Tie the rocket to the ribbon so that it hangs down from the centre of the mobile.

Pig & Piglet

No playpen would be complete without this heavyweight pair! Featuring floppy ears and the large one with a couple of brown spots on her back, plump piggies like this could only be stitched in chunky yarn.

FINISHED SIZE
Pig: 42 × 22 cm (16½ × 8¾ in)
Piglet: 15 × 8 cm (6 × 3 in)

MATERIALS
- **Karabella** *Aurora Bulky*
  One ball of Shell Pink 9 (MC)
- **Debbie Bliss** *Cashmerino Aran*
  Small amount of Pink 04-04 (A)
- **GGH** *Velour*
  Small amount of Chocolate 05 (B)
- **Rooster** *Almerino DK*
  One ball of Strawberry Cream 203 (C)
  Small amount of Caviar 206 (D)
- Grey, blue and cream yarn for eyes
- Dark brown yarn for mouth
- Hook: 8.00 mm (L-11), 6.50 mm (K-10½) and 4.00 mm (G-6)
- Polyester toy fibrefill or wadding
- Yarn needle

TENSION
7 sts and 6 rows measured over 5 cm (2 in), working double crochet in MC and using 6.50 mm (K-10½) hook.

NOTE:
Before beg the second rnd in each section, place a marker or short length of contrasting yarn across your crochet and up against the loop on the hook and above the working yarn. Work Rnd 2, then slip the marker out and place it at the beg of the next rnd and so on. The marker will indicate where each subsequent rnd starts.

Pig

HEAD & BODY
Foundation row: Using yarn MC and 8.00 mm (L-11) hook, beg at the snout, make 2ch.
Rnd 1: 6dc in second ch from hook.
Rnd 2: 2dc in each of next 6dc (12 dc).
Rnd 3: *1dc in next dc, 2dc in next dc, rep from * around (18 dc).
Rnd 4: 1dc in each of next 18dc.
Change to 6.50 mm (K-10½) hook, rep last rnd 4 times more.
Shape top of head
Rnd 9: 2dc in each of next 9dc, 1dc in each of next 9dc (27 dc).
Rnd 10: [1dc in next dc, 2dc in next dc] 9 times, 1dc in each of next 9dc (36 dc).
Rnd 11: 1dc in each of next 36dc.
Shape chin
Rnd 12: 1dc in each of next 27dc, [2dc in next dc, 1dc in next dc] 4 times, 1dc in last dc (40 dc).
Rnd 13: 1dc in each of next 40dc.
Rep last rnd 3 times more.
Shape head
Rnd 17: [1dc in each of next 4dc, miss next dc, 1dc in each of next 3dc, miss next dc] 4 times, 1dc in each of next 3dc, miss next dc (31 dc).
Rnd 18: [1dc in each of next 6dc, miss next dc] 3 times, 1dc in each of next 10dc (28 dc).
Change to 8.00 mm (L-11) hook.
Rnd 19: 1dc in each of next 28dc.
Rep last rnd twice more.
Rnd 22: [1dc in each of next 2dc, miss next dc] 6 times, 1dc in each of next 10dc (22 dc).
Rnd 23: 1dc in each of next 4dc, 2dc in each of next 14dc, 1dc in each of next 4dc (36 dc).
Rnd 24: 1dc in each of next 36dc.
Rep last rnd until the head and body measure 33 cm (13 in) from snout to back end.
Stuff the snout, head and body.
Next rnd: *1dc in each of next 2dc, miss next dc, rep from * around until the gap closes.

Make 15ch for the tail, twist it to curl it a little, fasten off.

LARGE SPOT

Foundation row: Using yarn D and 4.00 mm (G-6) hook, make 2ch.
Rnd 1: 6dc in second ch from hook.
Rnd 2: 2dc in each of next 6dc (12 dc).
Rnd 3: *1dc in next dc, 2dc in next dc, rep from * around (18 dc).**
Rnd 4: *1dc in each of next 2dc, 2dc in next dc, rep from * around (24 dc).
Rnd 5: *1dc in each of next 3dc, 2dc in next dc, rep from * around (30 dc).
Rnd 6: *1dc in each of next 4dc, 2dc in next dc, rep from * around, ending with sl st in top of next dc (36 dc).
Fasten off.

SMALL SPOT

Work as for large spot up to **, ending with sl st in top of next dc.
Fasten off.

EARS

Make 2 alike.
Foundation row: Using yarn A and 8.00 mm (L-11) hook, beg at the top of the ear, make 17ch.
Row 1: 1dc in second ch from hook, 1dc in each of next 12ch, miss next ch, 1dc in last ch, turn (14 dc).
Row 2: 1ch, miss first dc, 1dc in each of next 11dc, miss next dc, 1dc in last dc, turn (12 dc).
Row 3: 1ch, miss first dc, 1dc in each of next 9dc, miss next dc, 1dc in last dc, turn (10 dc).
Row 4: 1ch, miss first dc, 1dc in each of next 7dc, miss next dc, 1dc in last dc, turn (8 dc).
Row 5: 1ch, miss first dc, 1dc in each of next 5dc, miss next dc, 1dc in last dc, turn (6 dc).
Row 6: 1ch, miss first dc, 1dc in each of next 3dc, miss next dc, 1dc in last dc, turn (4 dc).
Fasten off.

HIND LEGS

Make 2 alike.
Foundation row: Using yarn MC and 6.50 mm (K-10½) hook, beg at the base of the trotter, make 2ch.
Rnd 1: 6dc in second ch from hook.
Rnd 2: 2dc in each of next 6dc (12 dc).
Rnd 3: 1dc in each of next 12dc, sl st in top of first dc (12 dc).
Join in yarn B to same place as sl st was worked.
Rnd 4: 1dtr in each of next 12dc (12 dtr).
Rnd 5: 1dtr in each of next 12dtr, sl st in top of first dtr.
Rnd 6: Join in yarn MC in same place as sl st was worked, 1dc in each of next 12dtr (12 dc).

Rnd 7: 1dc in each of next 12dc.
Shape front of leg
Rnd 8: 1dc in each of next 3dc, [1dc in next dc, 2dc in next dc] 3 times, 1dc in each of next 3dc (15 dc).**
Rnd 9: 1dc in each of next 4dc, 2dc in each of next 7dc, 1dc in each of next 4dc (22 dc).
Rnd 10: 1dc in each of next 22dc.
Rep last rnd twice more. Fasten off.

FORELEGS

Make 2 alike.
Work as for hind leg up to **.
Rnd 9: 1dc in each of next 15dc.
Rep last rnd once more. Fasten off.

TO FINISH

Sew the ears in place with a decreasing row edge oversewn onto the top of the head. Around the top edge of the snout, between rows 2 and 4, sew a backstitch line to shape the rim of the snout.

Sew four short rows of grey yarn together to create the eyes. Onto this, sew a French knot in a small length of cream yarn. Make 10ch in a short length of blue yarn and sew around the grey. Sew a mouth across the bottom of the snout using a length of dark brown yarn.

Sew on the spots with WS facing up. Sew on the hind legs with front facing forward, leaving a gap for stuffing. Stuff the legs then sew up the gap. Sew on the forelegs with front facing you, stuff as before.

Piglet

Make all in one piece.

Foundation row: Using yarn C and 4.00 mm (G-6) hook, beg at the snout, make 4ch.

Row 1: 2dc in second ch from hook, 1dc in next ch, 2dc in last ch, turn (5 dc).

Row 2: 1ch, 2dc in first dc, 1dc in each dc to last dc, 2dc in last dc, turn (7 dc). Rep last row 4 times more (15 dc).

Row 7: 1ch, 1dc in each of next 15dc, make 7ch for first front leg, turn.

Row 8: 1dc in second ch from hook, 1dc in each of next 5ch, 1dc in each of next 15dc, make 7ch for second front leg, turn.

Row 9: 1dc in second ch from hook, 1dc in each of next 5ch, 1dc in each of next 21dc, turn (27 dc).

Row 10: 1ch, 1dc in each of next 27dc, turn.

Rep last row twice more.

Row 13: 1ch, 1dc in each of next 21dc, turn.

Row 14: 1ch, 1dc in each of next 15dc, turn.

Rep last row 3 times more.

Row 18: 1ch, 1dc in each of next 15dc, make 7ch for first back leg, turn.

Row 19: 1dc in second ch from hook, 1dc in each of next 5ch, 1dc in each of next 15dc, make 7ch for second back leg, turn.

Row 20: 1dc in second ch from hook, 1dc in each of next 5ch, 1dc in each of next 21dc, turn (27 dc).

Row 21: 1ch, 1dc in each of next 27dc, turn.

Rep last row twice more.

Row 24: 1ch, 1dc in each of next 21dc, turn.

Row 25: 1ch, 1dc in each of next 15dc. Fasten off.

EARS

Make 2 alike.

Foundation row: Using yarn C and 4.00 mm (G-6) hook, beg at the base of the ear, make 6ch.

Row 1: 1dc in second ch from hook, 1dc in each of next 4ch, turn (5 dc).

Row 2: 1ch, 1dc in each of next 5dc, turn. Rep last row twice more.

Row 5: 1ch, miss first dc, 1dc in each of next 2dc, miss next dc, 1dc in last dc, turn (3 dc).

Row 6: 1ch, 1dc in each of next 3dc, turn.

Row 7: 1ch, miss first 2dc, 1dc in last dc. Fasten off.

TO FINISH

With RS facing and using matching yarn and backstitch throughout, fold in half across short row ends, sew around each leg, turn the legs out. Place body and head RS facing, sew along the bottom. Sew along the snout and under the chin, up to first pair of legs. Turn out. Stuff the legs a little, stuff the head and body, sew up the belly.

Using yarn C, make 10ch, join into a ring with a sl st in first ch, fasten off. Sew onto the end of the snout.

Sew the ears in place with base edge sewn onto the top of the head.

Using yarn C, make 10ch, twist the length of crochet, fasten off. Sew one end onto the back of the piglet for the tail.

Using grey yarn, sew the eyes onto the head with straight stitches.

Clover Cow & Calf

Moo-licious! Mummy and her wee one make a lovely pair when out to pasture or in your child's room. Clover boasts a striking all-over black-and-white pattern that's accented with pink. Her calf, still wobbly on all fours, makes a fine finger puppet as well!

FINISHED SIZES
Cow: 19 cm (7½ in) long × 10 cm (4 in) wide
Calf: 11 cm (4½ in) long × 6.5 cm (2½ in) wide

MATERIALS
- **Debbie Bliss** *Cashmerino Aran*
  One ball of Black 300300 (A)
  One ball of White 101 (MC)
- **Jaeger** *Pure Cotton DK*
  Small amount of Light Pink 0576 for nose and udder (B)
- Hook: 5.00 mm (H-8)
- Black sewing thread for attaching beads
- Two 6 mm (¼ in) black glass beads or similar for cow's eyes
- Polyester toy fibrefill or wadding
- Yarn needle

TENSION
12 sts and 9 rnds measured over 5 cm (2 in), working double crochet in MC and using 5.00 mm (H-8) hook.

NOTE:
Before beg the first rnd in each section, place a marker or short length of contrasting yarn across your crochet and up against the loop on the hook and above the working yarn. Work Rnd 2, then slip the marker out and place it at the beg of the next rnd and so on. The marker will indicate where each subsequent rnd starts.

Cow

HEAD & BODY
Using yarn B, beg at the nose end, make 3ch.
Foundation rnd: Working over tail end, 8dc in third ch from hook, join to top of 3ch with sl st to form ring (8 dc).
Rnd 1: 1dc in each of next 8dc.
Rnd 2: 2dc in each of next 8dc (16 dc).
Rnd 3: 1dc in each of next 16dc.
Rep last rnd 3 times more, ending with sl st in top of last dc of rnd.
Rnd 7: Join in yarn A to same place as sl st was worked, 1dc in each of next 16dc.
Rnd 8: 1dc in each of next 16dc.
Rep last rnd 5 times more, ending with sl st in top of first dc.

Fasten off, leaving the marker in the crochet so that you can pick up from there after sewing on face markings.
Add on face markings
Using yarn MC, make 24ch, leaving a long tail end for sewing.
Fasten off.
To sew on the face, thread up one end and secure it at the back of the cow's head.
Curl the chain into a circular shape that resembles the shape in the photograph, catching chain every so often to secure in place.
Referring to the photograph, sew on the nostrils with black yarn, working a couple of straight stitches for each nostril.
Cont with the body
Rejoin yarn A to sl st at end of last rnd on main body.
Shape neck
Rnd 14: *1dc in each of next 3dc, miss next dc, rep from * around (12 dc).
Rnd 15: 1dc in each of next 12dc.
Rnd 16: *1dc in next dc, 2dc in next, rep from * around (18 dc).
Rep last rnd once more (27 dc).

Rnd 18: 1dc in each of next 27dc.
Rep last rnd once more.

Shape belly

Rnd 20: [1dc in each of next 2dc, 2dc in next dc] twice, 1dc in each of next 15dc, [1dc in each of next 2dc, 2dc in next dc] twice (31 dc).

Rnd 21: 1dc in each of next 31dc.
Rep last rnd 16 times more, ending with sl st in top of first dc.
Fasten off, leaving the marker in the crochet so that you can pick up from there after sewing on body markings.

Add on body markings

Using yarn MC, make 50ch, leaving a long loose end for sewing with. Fasten off.
To sew on the body markings, thread up one end and secure it at the back of the cow's body, near the back end.
Curl the chain into a shape that resembles the shape in the photograph, catching chain every so often to secure in place.
Make a second shape with 70ch to sew onto the body near the neck.

Cont with the body

Rejoin yarn A to sl st at end of last rnd on main body.

Shape bottom

Rnd 38: *1dc in each of next 5dc, miss next dc, rep from * to last dc, miss last dc (25 dc).

Rnd 39: *1dc in each of next 4dc, miss next dc, rep from * around (20 dc).

Rnd 40: *1dc in each of next 3dc, miss next dc, rep from * around (15 dc).
Stuff the cow through the bottom.

Rnd 41: *1dc in each of next 2dc, miss next dc, rep from * around (10dc).

Rnd 42: *1dc in next dc, miss next dc, rep from * around until ring is closed.
Fasten off.

TAIL

Using yarn A, make 7ch, join in yarn MC and make 9ch. Fasten off, weaving in the yarn – leave the black tail end for sewing onto the body.
Using yarn MC, make a fringed end at the back (see instructions for fringing technique on page 82).

EARS

Make 2 alike.
Using yarn A, make 16ch.

Row 1: 1dc in second ch from hook, 1dc in each ch across (15 dc).
Fasten off yarn A, join in yarn B.

Row 2: 1dc in each of next 15dc.
Fasten off.

HORNS

Make 2 alike.
Using yarn MC, make 4ch.

Row 1: 1dc in third ch from hook, 1dc in next ch.

Fasten off, leaving the tail ends for sewing onto the head.

BLACK LEGS

Make 3 alike.
Beg with the hoof, using yarn A, make 3ch.

Foundation chain: Working over tail end, 8dc in third ch from hook (8 dc).

Rnd 1: 1dc in each of next 8dc.

Shape sides of hoof

Rep last rnd twice more.

Shape leg

Rnd 4: *1dc in each of next 3dc, miss next dc, rep from * once more (6 dc).

Rnd 5: 1dc in each of next 6dc.**
Rep last rnd until leg measures 10 cm (4 in) from hoof.
Fasten off, leaving the tail ends for sewing onto the body.

BLACK & WHITE LEG

Work as for black leg up to **.

Rnd 6: Join in yarn MC, 1dc in each of next 2dc, change to yarn A to complete the rnd.

Rnd 7: In yarn MC, 1dc in each of next 3dc, change to yarn A to complete rnd.

Rnd 8: In yarn MC, 1dc in each of next 4dc, change to yarn A to complete rnd.

Rnd 9: In yarn MC, 1dc in each of next 5dc, change to yarn A to complete rnd.
Fasten off yarn A.

Rnd 10: In yarn MC, 1dc in each of next 6dc.

Rep last rnd until leg measures 10 cm (4 in) from hoof.

Fasten off, leaving the tail ends for sewing onto the body.

UDDER

Foundation row: Using yarn B, make 2ch.

Rnd 1: 10dc in 2nd ch from hook (10 dc).

Rnd 2: 2dc in each dc around (20 dc).

Rnd 3: 1dc in each dc around.

Rep last rnd 3 times more.

Fasten off, pull up the loose end at the start to close the ring.

For the teats, cut four lengths of yarn B 10 cm (4 in) long. Secure the ends to the inside of the udder, thread through to the front at the foundation row, and let the threads dangle on the right side. Trim them to 10 cm (⅜ in) from udder.

TO FINISH

Stuff the legs lightly. Using a blunt-ended yarn needle and MC yarn, sew the four legs to the underside of the body equidistant from each other.

Sew each ear together, bending in half widthways, and joining the pink finishing row.

Sew the base of each ear in place, referring to the photograph for accurate positioning.

Sew the widest end of the horns to the top of the head in between the ears.
Sew on a glass bead at either side of the head for the eyes.
Sew the udder to the underside of the cow, about 2.5 cm (1 in) away from the bottom, stuffing it a little before completing the sewing.
Sew the cow's tail to its bottom.

Calf

HEAD & BODY

Foundation chain: Using yarn MC and beg at the tail end, make 9ch, join with sl st in first ch to form a ring, taking care not to twist the loop.
Rnd 1: 1dc in each of next 9ch (9 dc).
Rnd 2: *1dc in each of next 2ch, 2dc in next dc, rep from * around (12 dc).
Rnd 3: *1dc in each of next 3dc, 2dc in next dc, rep from * around (15 dc).
Tie yarn A to working yarn, and work it with yarn MC along the back of the work until it is needed.
Rnd 4: In MC 1dc in each of next 4dc, in yarn A 1dc in each of next 2dc, in MC 1dc in each of next 9dc.
Rnd 5: In MC 1dc in each of next 2dc, in yarn A 1dc in each of next 6dc, in MC 1dc in each of next 7dc.
Rnd 6: In MC 1dc in next dc, in yarnA 1dc

in each of next 8dc, in MC 1dc in each of next 6dc.
Rnd 7: In MC 1dc in each of next 2dc, in yarn A 1dc in each of next 6dc, in MC 1dc in each of next 7dc.
Rnd 8: In MC 1dc in each of next 4dc, in yarn A 1dc in each of next 2dc, in MC 1dc in each of next 9dc.
Break off yarn A and weave it into the back of the work, cont in yarn MC only.
Rnd 9: 1dc in each of next 15dc.
Rep last rnd 3 times more.
Shape head
Rnd 13: *1dc in each of next 2dc, miss next dc, rep from * around (10 dc).
Rnd 14: 1dc in each dc around.
Rnd 15: *1dc in next dc, miss next dc, rep from * around (5 dc).
Rnd 16: 1dc in each dc around.
Rep last rnd 5 times more.
Rnd 22: *1dc in next dc, miss next dc, rep from * around, rep until ring closes.
Fasten off, weave in end.
For the pink disc at the end of the nose, using yarn B, make 2ch, 7dc in 2nd ch from hook, ending sl st in top of first dc.
Fasten off.

EARS

Make 2 alike.
Foundation chain: Using yarn MC, make 6ch, fasten off.

TAIL

Foundation chain: Using yarn MC, make 10ch, fasten off.
Make a fringed end with 3 lengths of yarn, trimmed to 12 mm (½ in) afterwards (see instructions for fringing technique on page 82).

LEGS

Make 4 alike.
Foundation chain: Using yarn MC, make 9ch.
Row 1: 1dc in second ch from hook, 1dc in each ch across, turn (8dc).
Row 2: 1ch, 1dc in each dc across, turn.
Fasten off.

TO FINISH

Sew up the seam at the back of the legs, then, with yarn A sew on a couple of straight stitches at each side of the foot for hooves.
With your finger in the puppet, taking care not to pinch yourself, sew on the two ears joining both ends. Sew on two eyes, stitching a French knot for each with the black yarn. Sew the pink disk to the end of the nose.
Sew on the tail and the legs.

Techniques & Abbreviations

Crochet abbreviations

alt	alt
approx	approximately
beg	beginning
ch	chain(s)
ch sp	chain space(s)
cm	centimetre(s)
cont	continue
dc	double crochet
dc2tog	double crochet two stitches together
dc3tog	double crochet three stitches together
dec	decrease
dtr	double treble
foll	following
htr	half treble crochet
in	inch(es)
inc	increase
m	metre(s)
mm	millimetre(s)
oz	ounce(s)
patt(s)	pattern(s)
rem	remaining
rep	repeat
RS	right side
sp	space(s)
ss2tog	slip stitch two stitches together
sl st	slip st
st(s)	stitch(es)
tch	turning chain
tog	together
tr	treble
trtr	triple treble
WS	wrong side
yd	yard(s)
yo	yarn over hook (US)
yrh	yarn around hook
[ ]	work instructions in square brackets as directed

Hook conversion

US size	Metric	Old UK/CAN size
–	2.00	14
B/1	2.25	13
–	2.50	12
C/2	2.75	–
–	3.00	11
D/3	3.25	10
E/4	3.50	9
F/5	3.75	–
6	4.00	8
7	4.50	7
H/8	5.00	6
I/9	5.50	5
J/10	6.00	4
K101⁄2	6.50	3
11	7.00	2
L/12	8.00	0
M/13	9.00	00
N/15	10.00	000
P/16	16.00	–
S	19.00	–

Useful stitches

Backstitch

Use for sewing strong seams or for attaching trims by hand. Bring the needle up from the underside of the fabric and insert it about 3 mm (1⁄8 in) behind the point at which the thread came out. Bring the needle out about 3 mm (1⁄8 in) in front of the starting point. Continue in same manner.

French Knot

Bring the needle out on the surface of the fabric at the place where the knot is to lie. Wrap the thread around the needle two or three times, depending on how big you want the knot to be. Insert the needle close to where it came out. Holding the knot in place, pull the needle to the wrong side to secure the knot.

Oversew

Sew the two edges together with close stitches that pass over them both approximately 3 mm (1⁄8 in) from the edge of both edges.

Satin Stitch

Work parallel straight stitches, close together, across the entire area of a shape to fill it.

Stem Stitch

Bring the needle to the front at the left-hand side of the working line. With the thread beneath the needle, take it through to the back just beneath the working line. Pull the needle through. The thread at this point creates a very slight diagonal to the working line. Continue making these diagonal stitches along the working line, keeping all the stitches the same size.

Yarn Information

ADRIAFIL
- **Angora Carezza DK/ wool/nylon mix,** 50g/1¾oz ball, each approx 83m/90yd

ANCHOR
- **Tapisserie Wool,** 5g/⅙oz skein, each approx 10m/11yd

ARTESANO
- **Alpaca,** 50g/1¾oz ball, each approx 83m/90yd

BERGERE DE FRANCE
- **Doussine,** 50g/1¾oz ball, each approx 160m/174yd

BROWN SHEEP COMPANY
- **Cotton Fleece,** 113g/4oz ball, each approx 238m/215yd
- **Lambs Pride Worsted,** 113g/4oz ball, each approx 174m/190yd

COTTAGE KNITS
- **Chenille,** 50g/1¾oz ball, each approx 92m/100yd

DEBBIE BLISS YARNS
- **Baby Cashmerino,** 50g/1¾oz ball, each approx 125m/136yd
- **Cashmerino Aran,** 50g/1¾oz ball, each approx 90m/98yd
- **Cashmerino Astrakhan,** 50g/1¾oz ball, each approx 70m/76yd
- **Cashmerino Chunky,** 50g/1¾oz ball, each approx 70m/76yd
- **Cotton Denim Aran,** 50g/1¾oz ball, each approx 68m/74yd

FROG TREE
- **Chunky,** 50g/1¾oz ball, each approx 50m/54yd

GGH
- **Big Easy,** 50g/1¾oz ball, each approx 71m/77yd
- **Samoa-Mouline,** 50g/1¾oz ball, each approx 95m/104yd

JAEGER
- **Aqua Cotton,** 50g/1¾oz ball, each approx 106m/116yd
- **Baby Merino 4-ply,** 50g/1¾oz ball, each approx 183m/200yd
- **Natural Fleece,** 50g/1¾oz ball, each approx 85m/93yd
- **Pure Cotton DK,** 50g/1¾oz ball, each approx 106m/116yd
- **Roma,** 50g/1¾oz ball, each approx 125m/137yd

JO SHARP YARNS
- **Kid Mohair,** 50g/1¾oz ball, each approx 87m/95yd

KARABELLA
- **Aurora Bulky,** 50g/1¾oz ball, each approx 51m/56yd
- **Vintage Cotton,** 50g/1¾oz ball, each approx 92m/100yd
- **Vintage Mercerized Cotton,** 50g/1¾oz ball, each approx 130m/140yd

KING COLE
- **Merino Blend DK,** 50g/1¾oz ball, each approx 112m/124yd

LOBSTER POT
- **Bulky,** 100g/3½ oz ball, each approx 106m/115yd

LOUISA HARDING
- **Kashmir DK,** 50g/1¾oz ball, each approx 119m/130yd

OPAL
- **Uni 4-ply,** 50g/1¾oz ball, each approx 425m/460yd

ROOSTER
- **Almerino DK,** 50g/1¾oz ball, each approx 112.5m/124yd

ROWAN
- **All Seasons Cotton,** 50g/1¾oz ball, each approx 90m/97.5yd
- **Big Wool,** 50g/1¾oz ball, each approx 80m/87yd
- **Kid Silk Haze,** 50g/1¾oz ball, each approx 210m/229yd
- **Lurex Shimmer,** 50g/1¾oz ball, each approx 95m/104yd
- **Soft Baby,** 50g/1¾oz ball, each approx 150m/164yd
- **Summer Tweed Aran,** 50g/1¾oz ball, each approx 108m/118yd
- **4-ply Cotton,** 50g/1¾oz ball, each approx 170m/186yd

Yarn Resources

RYC
- **Cashcotton 4-ply**, 50g/1¾oz ball, each approx 180m/197yd
- **Cashsoft 4-ply**, 50g/1¾oz ball, each approx 180m/197yd
- **Cashsoft Aran**, 50g/1¾oz ball, each approx 87m/95yd
- **Cashsoft DK (light worsted)**, 50g/1¾oz ball, each approx 130m/142yd
- **Luxury Cotton DK**, 50g/1¾oz ball, each approx 95m/104yd
- **Silk Wool DK**, 50g/1¾oz ball, each approx 100m/109yd

SIRDAR
- **Bonus Chunky**, 100g/3½oz ball, each approx 137m/149yd
- **Breeze**, 50g/1¾oz ball, each approx 264m/288yd
- **Chunky**, 50g/1¾oz ball, each approx 58m/64yd
- **Snuggly DK**, 50g/1¾oz ball, each approx 276m/249yd

TWILLEYS
- **Freedom Cotton DK**, 50g/1¾oz ball, each approx 50m/55yd

ADRIAFIL
c/o www.plymouthyarn.com

ANCHOR
c/o www.westminsterfibers.com

ARTESANO
www.artesano.co.uk

BERGERE DE FRANCE
c/o www.angelyarns.com

BROWN SHEEP COMPANY
www.brownsheep.com

COTTAGE KNITS
www.cottageknits.com

DEBBIE BLISS
c/o www.knittingfever.com

FROG TREE
c/o www.kyarns.com

GGH
c/o www.muenchyarns.com

JAEGER
See Anchor

JO SHARP
www.josharp.com.au

KARABELLA
www.karabellayarns.com

KING COLE
www.kingcole.co.uk

LOBSTER POT
c/o www.kyarns.com

OPAL
www.ptyarn.com

ROOSTER
www.roosteryarns.com

ROWAN
See Anchor

RYC
See Anchor

SIRDAR
See Debbie Bliss

TWILLEYS
www.twilleys.co.uk

Acknowledgements

I would like to extend a huge thank you to Michelle Lo and Katie Cowan for inviting me to do this book, and lighting my creative flair!

Also, a huge thank you to the wonderful team at Collins & Brown, in particular Gemma Wilson, Ben, Ruth, Mark Winwood for his ability to make toys come to life, Amy, Komal, Joanna and Laura. A special big cheer for kindly Katie Hudson, with her gentle liaising and infectious enthusiasm.

It is really great to know and work with you all.